# Professional Pet Sitting for Love & Money

## By Jeff Grognet, DVM, BSc(Agr)

Professional Pet Sitting for Love & Money
By Jeff Grognet, DVM, BSc(Agr)
Copyright 2014 by Jeff Grognet

1. pet sitting

ISBN 13: 978-0-9937107-0-4

Jeff Grognet is a veterinarian practicing in Qualicum Beach, British Columbia, Canada. He has several courses for veterinary assistants and one for pet sitters through

`veterinaryassistantlearningcenter.com`

He is also a principal of the ACE Academy for Canine Instructors Inc. an organization that provides certification courses for students on canine obedience training and remedies for behavioral problems. It can be found at:

ACE Academy for Canine Educators Inc.

`dogtraining.academy`

# TABLE OF CONTENTS

# Introduction

Do you love working with animals? Are your best memories of quiet moments with a four-legged friend? Do you want a career following your passion? Pet sitting could be the ideal way to combine your love for animals with a paying profession.

This book is the only one you'll need to guide you in creating your own pet sitting business. Take a look at the table of contents and you'll see why. This book can be used alone or in conjunction with the on-line course "Start a Pet Sitting Business" offered on my website veterinaryassistantlearningcenter.com and through over 2300 colleges.

I have been in the "animal industry" for over 30 years. As a veterinarian, I see the tremendous bond between people and their pets. This is most often dogs and cats, but it can also be other furry, scaly, and feathered friends anyone loves.

In the last two decades, we've seen a new profession blossom, and that is pet sitting. The reason is simple - owners don't want to put their friends into kennels. They don't want to drop them off in a sterile concrete compartment that is supposed to be their dog's home for the next days or weeks. Instead, they want them to stay in the comfort of home and be cared for. Or, maybe the owners can't get home in the middle of the day and they want someone to let their cherished pooch out.

Pet sitting is a career that you can get into with minimal inputs and investment. It doesn't cost much financially. You can also start part-time and let it grow to a full-time career. Or, you can build such a progressive company that you are managing employees and making considerable income. The beauty is that you decide when and how much you want to work.

You can join this profession as long as you have love for animals, the commitment to get things done, and the knowledge. You have to supply the first two. I can help you with the knowledge.

## Someone Will Pay me to do This?

People hire pet sitters to look after their pets while they aren't at home. They may be at work, on vacation, or away for a weekend.

The reason people use pet sitters is because they want the best care for their pets. Boarding kennels are an alternative and they keep pets safe. But, they can't measure up to the one-on-one care a pet sitter supplies. In fact, and this is good for you, many owners now feel guilty putting their pets in kennels.

Doggy daycares look after dogs during the work day. Some dogs have a ball at these places, but if you have a timid or aggressive dog, it may not be the best solution. And, they close their doors at the end of every day, ending their care.

Pet sitters provide a unique service. They allow pets to stay home in familiar surroundings, providing personal care. As a pet sitter, you walk the dog and play with the cat. This gives you a chance to observe them. You are the early warning system to tell if a health issue is developing. And, you look after the home.

The greatest value I see in pet sitters is when they look after pets with special needs. For example, if you have a client with an elderly dog that needs twice daily medication to keep his arthritis comfortable and his heart condition controlled, it is much better if he stays quiet at home. A kennel may be very stressful to these dogs (cats too).

Other companions needing special attention are those on temporary medication (such as ointments for ear infections, drops for eye conditions, and antibiotics for bladder infections), blind dogs that only know their way around home, and cats with diabetes that require regular insulin injections. Don't worry. I'll tell you how you can learn to give injections and manage health issues in pets as well.

Once your foot is in the client's door, you'll quickly find that they ask you to do other things besides looking after their pets. You'll be going to the house on a regular basis, so the client may ask you to bring in the mail, open and close curtains, turn lights on, and generally make it look like someone is still living there. Crime deterrence is a reason someone uses a pet sitter rather than a kennel. They don't want the house looking empty.

## What Does a Pet Sitter's Day Look Like?

You may ask what a typical pet sitting day entails. There is no typical day. They are all different. Let's start by seeing how you fit clients into your day.

You might have several clients away on holidays and you visit their homes twice a day, morning and night. You can fill the middle of the day with dogs and cats needing care while their owners are hard at work.

These clients might ask you to go to their house mid-day to let their pooch out and possibly provide a snack. Others want a late-afternoon visit because they will be late getting home.

Overnight service, when you stay in the client's home, is another thing you might want to offer, depending on your circumstances. With you there, the pet isn't left alone (important if a pet is epileptic or in poor shape). If something occurs, veterinary care can be arranged right away. Also, some people are extremely nervous about leaving their house empty. This type of care can complement your regular day duties.

What you will also find is that people that own pets don't stop at dogs and cats. They may also have exotic pets such as birds, reptiles, and little furry friends like hamsters and guinea pigs, or people with horses may want to use your services. It's up to you what animals you ultimately end up taking care of.

## Why be a Pet Sitter?

Never forget why you want to be a pet sitter. It is the animals. You get to spend time with furry friends, ensuring they get the best care. Some pet sitters don't even call what they do a job because they enjoy it so much.

Here is why you can feel good about being a pet sitter:

- You get to work with animals that you love.

- You help clients take good care of their pets and they will thank you for it. They don't feel guilty leaving their pet behind.

- And, you are the master and get to run the business the best way you can.

I bet you didn't know this—becoming a pet sitter seems to instantly make you an expert on animals. People see you as a person with knowledge and I can guarantee they will ask your advice. They may query you about exercise requirements for their new dog. They may quiz you on the best food for their cat. They may find something wrong with their pet and ask you if you recommend a veterinary visit. This is why learning all you can is so important. This book will do just that.

# The Pet Sitting Market

The pet sitter field is relatively new. The reason - society has changed! Years ago, pet owners just asked the neighbor's kid to feed their pets. These days, people don't know their neighbors well and kids are too busy to take on the responsibility.

People are also more concerned about security of their home—they want someone they can rely on when they hand over the keys. People tend to trust like-minded people. Because you like animals like they do, you fit the bill perfectly.

Years ago, paying someone to look after a pet was considered an extravagant luxury. But, pet care has come of age, just like the complicated, expensive procedures people now pay for in veterinary hospitals, pet sitting is not a luxury anymore, it is a necessity.

You are probably wondering if you can make a living by being a pet sitter. You can. In fact, as a pet sitter, you have an (almost) unlimited income potential. You can keep booking appointments until you fill your day. If you have too much work, you can turn some people away (just keep the clients you want), or you can hire employees to share the workload.

I'll get into what specific money you can earn and the plusses and minuses of employees later, but it all comes down to how much you want to work. Some pet sitters work part-time and take home $20,000 in a year. On the other hand, you can work very hard and push your income over $50,000 annually.

There is a huge number of animals creating opportunities for pet sitters. According to the American Pet Products Association 2013 survey, 47 percent of US households owned a dog. This made a total of 83.3 million dogs. There are even more cats—a total of 95.6 million, and each household with cats has 2.1 of them.

If you hadn't noticed, cats are taking over. Each year, we see proportionately more cats and fewer dogs. There are several theories for this, such as smaller homes and lifestyles that suit cats better. But, the point I want to make is that you need to keep this trend in mind. If you focus on dogs and ignore the growing feline market, you may be missing a significant income opportunity. I know from my experience, the shift from dogs to cats has had a major impact on the services offered in veterinary hospitals.

Are you interested in horses? Only 1.5 percent of households had one or more of these magnificent beasts, but each had an average of 2.7 horses. In 2012, there were just under 5.7 million horses in the US. According to statistics, the number of horses is slowly falling. There is a market for horse sitters, but you have to live in the right place.

These numbers show you the market you can tap into. Animal care is a growth industry, and people are spending more and more each year. It involves pet stores, veterinarians, and of course, pet sitters. These numbers are from the US, but the trends are similar no matter what country you live in.

Even better news for you is that people that own pets inevitably take a holiday or get called away from home for family issues or work travel. They need someone to look after their fur-kids.

What is the best place for a pet sitting business? It is the suburbs. People live there rather than the city because they want room for themselves and their pets. This means more pets per capita than you'd see in bigger cities, in apartments, or out in the country. People in the country are also farther apart, which is not ideal for you because that boosts your traveling costs dramatically.

People in the suburbs also have typical lifestyles. They likely commute to work and leave their pets at home all day. And, they go on vacations, traveling to exotic places. All this adds up to a need for pet sitters.

Interestingly, pet sitting clients tend to share common traits. People that want to hire you tend to be well educated with most having been to college or university. Most are upper wager-earners. They also work. They have a steady income and can afford to hire you.

Where I practice, there are lots of retired people. At first glance, they may not seem like the optimal clients because when they go on holidays, they tend to take their pets with them. And, if they leave Fido or Fluffy at home, they often have friends they depend on to look after them.

But, the pet sitters in my area tell me of the good points to retirees. They tend to book you well in advance so you can plan your work. The bonus is that they talk amongst themselves which means lots of free advertising. If you can crack the market, it can be lucrative.

If you want to set up a business, the first thing you need to do is to see if you have a large enough market. There are several ways to determine this.

Visit the local pet supply stores. Are they successful? Are any new stores being built? People in pet stores can give you their take on the need for pet sitting because people regularly ask them about pet services. If the pet store provides doggie day care or boarding, they probably won't want to reveal too much, but the fact they are there is positive.

Look for veterinary hospitals. The clients they service are the same ones you will be depending on. If there are several veterinary hospitals or a number of veterinarians at one hospital, there must be clients supporting them. Even better, these clients have already demonstrated that they take care of their pets.

Another source for information is the local Chamber of Commerce. They can't give you detailed information on your specific business, but they have a pulse on the community and you can certainly ask their opinion about launching a new enterprise.

Lastly, take a look around and see if there are any established pet sitters. Look in the phone book, on the Internet, or ask at any of the "pet places" I've listed above.

But, don't think that the existence of a pet sitter stops you from opening your own business. In fact, the presence of another pet sitter shows there is a market. As a plus, you may be able to get referrals from the other pet sitter businesses by saying you are available – you can help them out when they are busy. If there are no pet sitters, take a real close look. There may be a reason. Or, it may just be an untapped market.

Boarding kennels also show you there is a need for someone to look after pets. Clients that use kennels might be willing to change to you, if you can make yourself attractive. Some dogs and cats get very stressed at kennels and pet sitters are a great alternative if they are older and need special care.

So, based on what we've covered so far, you can see that pet sitting —visiting, caring for, and walking pets—is thriving. You have probably identified several people you know that you can provide service to. I'll bet you've decided to go ahead with your plan, so let's see what you need to jump into the business.

# Getting Started in Pet Sitting

Pet sitting has several distinct advantages over other types of businesses. The biggest one is that you can start small with little investment. You can get going with a few business cards, a phone, and a way to get around.

You can make the cards on your home computer. You can use the phone that you carry in your pocket. And transportation is usually a car, but if you live in a city, busses may be an option. You don't need an office other than a corner in your home and you don't have to stock inventory.

The wonderful thing about pet sitting is that you can keep your business small, working limited hours, or grow it as big as you want. You may want to just work during the day while your kids are in school. If you are a student, you can work before and/or after school. You are the boss, so you decide how much you want to work, and when.

There are two essential traits you need to be a pet sitter, but I bet you already have them. One is a love for animals. You can't be a pet sitter without liking the dogs and cats you are looking after.

I'll tell you about the love I mean. Let's say you see a lost dog in the park. Are you the one that runs after the little fellow, getting wet in the rain and being late for work, just so he can be reunited with his parents? If you see a cat up a tree, are you the one that climbs the ladder even though you are scared of heights?

Here's my story. I've been working recently creating a dog instruction training course. Because of this, I'm seeing lots of dogs. At times, you'll see me on the floor, playing with the puppies, just enjoying their energy. I can get lost doing that and I'm sure it can calm anyone down. Similarly, if I'm on the couch reading and my cat Calvin decides that I'm not allowed to read anymore and he has to lie on me, I fall for it every time.

Love for animals is one trait. Can you guess what the other is?

It is being responsible. You cannot succeed if you are not willing to take on the responsibility. When you arrange an appointment and clients are depending on you, or more specifically Hudson the Lab is waiting for you to let him out to go pee, you have to keep it. Missing an appointment is not allowed. And, you have to be committed – you can't go on holidays at a moment's notice. If you aren't dependable, clients will drop you.

Just think of the faith they must have in you when they hand over the keys to their homes and access to all the contents in them. It is a huge responsibility.

Another thing to consider when looking at being a pet sitter is that you can specialize. You can have a feline-only pet sitting business if you prefer cats. If you like exercise and walking, you can concentrate on dog-owning clients. If you are physically challenged, you may want to limit your pet sitting to cats or small dogs. If you have an expertise in horses, look for work with the equines.

If you live in a seniors' community, chances are you'll be seeing small dogs and cats. Most of these owners don't want to send their cherished little four-leggeds to a kennel. People living in apartments would also favor cats. This is where knowing your market is so important.

The other plus of starting as a pet sitter is that it takes little training. You do need to know how to look after dogs and cats. This may come naturally to you because you've been around animals all your life. But, it changes when you are looking after someone else's pet and you are the one in charge of all decisions. All of a sudden, you need to know more. Because my focus is pet health, I will make sure you know how to spot problems and what to do.

In this book, you are going to learn the business of pet sitting. I'll show you how to make the best initial impression. Did you know that you sometimes should avoid a pet sitting gig? I'll tell you why. I've got forms for you to download on my website so you can gather the information you need.

Marketing can be a challenge, both doing it effectively and economically. You can use Facebook, websites, articles in the local paper, and each of these have their advantages and disadvantages. We'll look at insurance, hiring employees, and why you should look critically at bonding. We'll take a peak at accounting, and how to construct a business plan. Lastly, you'll discover what you can do to expand the business. It can be a lot of fun.

## First Impressions - The First Meeting

This initial contact is where you have to shine in your prospective client's eyes. You are selling your services and enticing the client to buy them. You need to look and act professional, and be organized.

Let's look at the purpose of the first meeting. This is the client's opportunity to meet you and judge you. This is also when you gather information on the pet and client, and delve into what services the client may be looking at purchasing from you.

Note that I said purchasing from you. You are in a service industry and you can never take the client for granted. You are not doing the client a favor by offering your services. She is doing you a favor by considering employing you. You have to convince her that you are the person to employ.

Let's go in-depth on the "first impression". This is so important, yet too many people don't appreciate what is involved in it. You need to dress well, use the right body language, and exude the confidence that you can do this job, and do it right.

How do you make the best impression? Put yourself in the client's shoes. She is looking for someone to care for her furchild. She is also trusting you with the keys to her home. Both of these take incredible faith in you. She wants someone who is responsible, professional, dependable, and trustworthy. Are you up to the challenge? Can you exude these traits?

Begin by looking in the mirror. I don't expect you to wear business attire (unless, of course, that is your normal dress), but look well groomed with smart but functional clothes. Some say that "business casual" is what you want. You can decide if you dress up for this interview or you wear your working clothes.

And, don't chew gum! I had a student come in for a job interview and she dressed well and seemed like a nice person, but throughout the interview, she chewed gum. And, I don't mean daintily. She was chewing it like a cow chewing her cud. I was so distracted by it that I found it hard to focus on what she was telling me. Did it influence my hiring decision? You bet!

Body language and attitude are important. Stay in the client's shoes and consider the following scenarios. You are now the pet sitter's potential employer.

During the meeting, Sheila the pet sitter never looks at you. She keeps her eyes down and refuses to make eye contact. You don't know if she is just shy or avoiding your gaze. Can you trust this person enough to leave your pet and home in her care?

Randy comes in and talks like your brother-in-law who sells cars. Your guard comes up when he says that his business is so successful and he is so busy that you need to make a decision today if you want to book him. If you don't, he can't guarantee he'll be available when you plan your holiday.

Stephanie seems like the "girl next door". She is interested in your dog, even petted him and let him kiss her. She is so nice, all you want to do is ask her if she wants a cup of tea.

Do you get the idea? Try to be the person you would hire. Of course, the best way to come across also depends on the client you are meeting. Is she a senior or is she 25 years old? See if you can figure out how you would talk to each of these clients to satisfy what they think is the ideal pet sitter.

The key to this meeting is being organized. Arrive early for the meeting. Clients want to see if you are punctual. If you do it once, they think you will do it each time you visit the home. If you are late, well, I think you can see what they are thinking. When you set up this meeting, book it 15 minutes later than you think you'll be free so that you won't be delayed.

Look and act like you know what you are doing. I'll outline what you do on a pet visitation later and that will help you develop a plan on what you can tell the client you do.

For now, show her how serious you are about taking the best care of their pet. Start by showing a genuine interest. As you ask these questions, you may want to tell them why you want this information. It shows you care about the job you do. By asking things, it tells them you care! The owner will feel like she is leaving her pets in responsible hands.

Call the pet by its name. This may seem like a small point, but it really sets up a bond between you and the pet, and with the owner. As well, try to get the pet's sex right and refer to him or her.

Talking about hims and hers, did you notice that I keep calling the client "her"? The reason I do this is that it is most likely going to be a woman who will be deciding if you are hired (or not).

## Topics for the First Meeting

What can you cover in your initial meeting? Start with easy questions and get comfortable with the client. Find out what pets are in the home. Their names? Age? Breed? Any interesting facts about them? Ask the client how she first met her dog/cat. This last one always gets clients talking.

Next, assess the client's needs. You need to figure out how often the client wants a visit. If you can, remind the client there is a fee each time you come by. Tell her how much it costs. We'll look at fees later.

Now, some details. Ask where the pet food is kept. Where are the pets fed? Where are the cleaning supplies? Pets can always make a mess and you'll want the house to look good when the owner comes back. What medications are the pets on?

Is there someone you can call in an emergency, both with a pet or with the house? Tell her that if the pet has a medical problem, you can recognize it. We'll cover this part, so you'll be able to do this. Ask her what veterinarian she prefers.

If there is a disaster in the home, what will you do? For example, if the furnace packs it in or the water pipes freeze, and it's January in Connecticut, will you get help or will there be someone to call?

Tell the client what happens in emergencies. For example, what happens if you are sick? If there is a snow storm, what is your contingency plan?

In the meeting, do not tell them how much better you are than other pet sitters. Doing that does not make you look good and it's unprofessional. Instead, depend on your qualities and skills to make you shine.

Another little idea for you is to put any certifications or training you have received on your brochure or in a folder to show the client. A completion letter from my pet sitting course can help show clients you are committed. References and testimonials from current clients can also go a long way to show people that you do a good job.

And most important, once you say you can provide the service, make sure you do it! Once the client has confidence in you, s/he will tell others, or you can use these clients as your references.

When you first get started, you will be doing a lot of these introductory meetings. Find ways to speed them up. Email or fax a form for the client to fill out. Ask them to have it ready when you arrive.

I've prepared several forms you can use or modify. If you have your own website, you can put the forms on it so that clients can download them.

## Practice Meeting

Find a friend who has cats or dogs. Tell them you are starting a pet sitting business and you want them to interview you just as if they were going to hire you. Of course, your livelihood won't be depending on this interview, but I want you to do it like it will be.

Prepare all the information you can to answer the questions you think will come up. Include everything you want to tell her. You want to finish the interview knowing that you have said everything that you wanted to. Take your notes with you if you have to.

The key is be prepared. It will take a lot of thought on what you want to say, but have fun while you are doing this. When you are done, review your experience. What did you do great and what could you have done better?

## Phone Etiquette

Often, the client initiates contact by phoning you. You may be able to answer the phone and talk, but always have a backup plan. Create a message that exudes professionalism. You can't just say "You've reached Monica, leave a message". No client will leave a message with that greeting. And don't use the one automatically generated by your phone company – it is as impersonal as you can get.

Instead, through your greeting, tell them who you are, what you do, and what will happen if they leave a message. Try a variation on this. "You have reached Furever Pet Sitting Services. This is Monica and I'm busy looking after one of my favorite pets. I'm sorry I've missed your call, but leave a message, and I'll call you as soon as I can." You can also ask people to tell you the best time you can call them back and at what number.

The simplest and most effective thing you can do to impress people is to return their calls. Taking a few days to return calls tells the customer one thing – they are not important in your eyes. If you are slow in returning calls, they may think you are never around or hard to reach if it's an urgent matter. If the call is from a client you are pet sitting for that day, call back immediately. And, a little thing such as knowing their pet's name when you call back can really put you in their good books.

If you want an appraisal of how you come across, ask a friend, or several, to act as clients and they can "interview" you. If you do it several times, the practice will get you comfortable with the flow of your answers and questions.

# The Financial Side of being a Pet Sitter.

Do you want to augment your income while working another job? Are you not working and just want to make a little money? In these situations, you may want to consider working part-time. You could donate just three hours a day to pet sitting. Or, is pet sitting going to be your full-time job and you're depending on it for all your income?

How much you work has a direct bearing on how many clients you can take on and this affects how much money you can make. The advantage of starting with just a few clients is that it will give you a taste of what the job entails. You can see if you truly like it before jumping in with both feet. You can also establish systems so you can become efficient. And, if you are hesitant about losing the security of a regular job, I recommend starting part-time.

But, if you are working, you can only do part-time and this depends on your current job being flexible, and it never calls you out of town on short notice. Also, suppose you went to look after Freddy the Dachshund before work and you found the little guy was sick. Can you afford to take the time to get him to a veterinarian and then go in to work? Suppose the worst happened – the same thing occurred three times over the next two weeks. How flexible/accommodating/nice is your employer?

Once you've got a taste of pet sitting and you find you thrive in your new career, and you ache to do more, you may want to put all your energy into pet sitting and go full-time. For some of you, this means leaving the security of a 9 to 5 job as well as the paycheck that goes along with it.

How fast you get into pet sitting depends on your circumstances – every person is different. For example, you may have a significant other that can support you. You may have another income source that can cover your expenses. Alternatively, you may have a lot in savings to help during the transition. The contrasting situation, and unfortunately far more common, is that you need to keep working until your pet sitting career starts to bring in some money.

## Your Financial Needs

Let's start by looking at your requirements. Some people can live well on $20,000 a year. Others require double that (or more). It depends on your life style and your goals. Be honest with yourself— what do you truly need?

Let's assume your plan is to become a full-time pet sitter, but you want to do it as well as your current job until it takes off. Let's also assume the job you plan to leave pays you $30,000 a year. I chose this number to make calculations easy. The boss has told you that you can reduce to half time (20 hours a week) any time you want. So, you decide to start pet sitting while still working and slowly re-place one job with another.

This is one way to do it. First, set your goal to take home $15,000 a year (half your current annual salary) from pet sitting while still working full-time. We'll get into accounting later, but let's assume you have $4,000 in annual expenses at that income level. This means you need to gross (bill to clients) $19,000 a year. As soon as you hit that $19,000 mark, you can drop your regular job to half time and your income stays the same.

I'll be the first to say that this won't be easy. Juggling pet sitting clients and working full-time will take great organization skills. It will also make it a long day. Some people find it better to drop their current job to two or three days a week or just work mornings while getting their business going.

But, if you've kept with the plan, now is the time to build it to the next level. If you need or want to maintain your income, you need $30,000 a year in take-home pay. This may mean you need to gross $38,000 (remember the expenses). Once you are doing this, or it's within striking distance, you can comfortably walk away from your job and your income stays the same.

The difference is that you are now your own boss and doing a job you love. But, it's also scary. You are dependent on YOU to generate the money. How do you do that?

As a pet sitter, most of your day is going to be spent visiting clients' homes. The first thing you want to do is set a fee for these visits.

## Setting Fees

One way to decide on what you charge is to do a survey. You may be able to find out what other pet sitters charge by doing some Internet research. You can also phone other pet sitters and ask. This gives you an idea what the range is.

But, something I must stress is – don't fall into the trap of matching them or trying to compete with them to attract clients. Why? Your business is going to be different! You are going to provide the best service possible and you should be paid for it.

The other argument is that if you undercut on fees, what type of clientele are you attracting? Do you want clients that will change pet sitters based on a few dollars a day? I can tell you about my experience with my practice. The clients that shop around based on cost (only) are not the clients that you want.

You want clients that love their pets and want the best care. You don't want the ones that settle for one visit a day when two are required for the pet's comfort.

Also, if you price yourself low, you'll need to run a larger volume through to make the same money. On the other hand, by pricing higher, you can provide exceptional service that merits the cost.

And, if you want to work with other pet sitters and enjoy a cordial relationship where you can periodically help each other out, you don't want to start by charging less and getting them upset.

As you can see, I suggest competing on service, not on price. But, these are only my thoughts. You may have compelling reasons to undercut the competition. For example, if you feel the other pet sitters are charging too much, you may want to compete on price as well as your quality.

Because every area is different, I can't tell you what to charge, but pet sitters in the US and Canada bill between $15 and $25 for each visit to a client's home. This is for a standard visit of about 30 minutes. If there is more than one pet, there is an additional charge. Some charge more for dogs than cats because it takes longer to care for a dog. There is also a premium for holidays, emergency visits, overnight visits, and pet transportation.

What you ultimately charge depends on how much driving you have to do between clients, the affluence of your neighborhood, do you have to pay for parking, and whether you are in a small town or big city (pet sitters tend to charge more in a big city).

Your financial needs do not affect how much you ultimately charge clients, but it does impact how hard you need to work.

## What can you make as a pet sitter?

Let's begin by assuming you charge $20 for each visit. Let's also assume it's a 30 minute visit. You'll find that you can quickly use this time up with a dog, but cats take less time (no need to take the cat for a walk). But, you have to get to the home or to the next client, so with traveling time, your visit actually takes about 45 minutes.

Can you do eight visits in a day? If you keep going (no break) this will take you 360 minutes, or six hours, and you gross $160. We are going to ignore expenses for now. We're just going to compare gross salaries.

Now, let's have some fun with numbers. Let's raise the per-visit fee to $25. With eight calls are making $200 per day. If we can add in two more visits, that's $250 total for just adding another hour and a half of work.

What can you do in a year? Let's stay at the $200 per day for easy calculations. How many days a week are you going to work? How many weeks holiday a year? This is another topic, but you do have to plan your holidays in advance and tell your clients or else they will book you and you are stuck at home. And, chances are you will be working every Christmas because your clients want to be away.

If you work five days a week and take two weeks off, you work 250 days a year. Maintaining a full schedule, at $200 per day, you could be grossing $50,000 a year. If you are a workaholic and work 300 days a year (one day a week off), you could hit $60,000. At $250 a day, that's $75,000. You won't be a millionaire, but it can be comfortable (but awfully busy). And, some pet sitters regularly receive tips which also boosts their income.

These numbers are based on a full schedule and this is not going to happen right away. We usually think that you will run at a loss (expenses will exceed your income) for the first three months while you are getting set up, and it will grow from there.

You may never reach the big figures because you won't want to (or can't) work that hard. Besides, you'll need to spend time interviewing clients to get them using your services. This will always be the case – you will lose some clients and need to replace them. It's impossible for every hour to be a billable hour.

It will also take time to reach your income goals. Clients aren't all going to phone at once and fill your schedule. They will get your information (from a brochure, website, or referral) and sit on it until they are planning a trip away. But, don't be discouraged. Just because the phone isn't ringing does not mean it won't. A reasonable time expectation to meet your income goals is a minimum of six months and more likely a year.

## Organizing yourself

Organization helps you be efficient with your time, but it also increases profits. The simplest way to begin is by looking at the order that you do your visits.

Try to arrange your stops so that you are covering the least distance, minimizing gas costs, and saving on travel time. You don't want to be backtracking and covering roads that you've already traveled on.

There are two ways to organize your visits. One is to write your appointments down on paper. For some, this is easy and accessible if you carry your appointment book with you. You can also create an electronic schedule with the many computer tools available. This is likely the better way to go when you have employees.

There are also many pet sitting software packages available to help you run a business. Some are free; others have a licensing fee with them.

The biggest challenge you are going to have is sorting out when you have business time and when you have personal time. You will find out quickly that you need time off. Of course, when you are starting out, you may want to work all your waking hours. But without a break, you will soon sour and not provide your clients with the exuberant happy, caring attitude or best quality work that you can be proud of.

If you want to work five days a week, plan on taking two mid-week days off. You are more likely to fill the weekends than weekdays with pet sitting appointments.

Of course, you are going to start out with just a few visits and build from there. You will quickly figure out what you can realistically do. Be kind to yourself so you can keep working.

Here's an idea to get you started, especially if you are worried about tackling your first client. Offer to look after your family and friends pets while they are away at a reduced rate. But, the key is to treat it like a real assignment. Do the client interview, fill out the forms, book the appointments as you set up your schedule, do the visits, and generate a bill to get paid. This will help you see the flow of what to do and what areas you need to work more on.

## When to say NO

I know you are just starting a business and probably hungry for clients, so it doesn't seem appropriate to talk about turning away a client. However, there are times you may want to do this. Two circumstances immediately come to mind – the last-minute requests and vicious dogs.

Suppose a client calls. They are leaving right away and need someone to quickly take responsibility for their pets. They want to leave the key under the mat and get to the airport. In fact, they are already on their way and you are not going to meet them.

Many pet sitters won't take these clients because they haven't had a chance to screen them. If the client can't take a few minutes to meet you, can you trust him/her? Will they pay the bill? Of course, this does not apply to the returning client that you know well. It's just the ones you don't know that you have to be wary about.

Also, from my experience at my veterinary hospital, the client that rushes in at the last minute and has never seen me before is not the best client. They demand more than the average client. And, if you do it once, they expect you to do the same next time. This said, some of these can be valuable, wonderful clients, and if they have a reference (someone refers them to you), perhaps you can take a second look.

If you decide you do want to take on these clients, get your information form filled out (they should be able to fill it out and fax or email it to you) so you have the details you need. If possible, arrange to meet them at their office to get the house key, and yes, you can charge a key pick-up fee.

Along the same lines are those clients that suck the time from you, what I call an "undesirable client". These are the ones that call you before they go away and explain, in excruciating detail, what to do at their home. A pet sitter I know told me of a client that insisted on showing her how to clean the litter box every time she went to pick up the key for the next assignment. And, this client also insisted on getting the key back so she had to go through with this with on every visit.

These time-wasters are also the ones that call once they are back asking you how their little fur-kid was, and they want to know everything! If a client is a pain and is simply asking too much of your time, you may want to consider dropping that client.

The other time not to accept a client is the vicious dog. I do not want you hurt. This is supposed to be a fun, safe job. If you find a dog too aggressive for you to handle or be comfortable with, consider walking away. Or, if the owner hands you a muzzle and tells you to put it on before the dog gets you, run away!

If you do want to take a job on that involves a questionable dog, get an emergency contact with the number of someone the dog knows just in case the dog won't let you in (or out of) the house. Your safety is a top priority.

The best clients, or ones that you should definitely accept are:

• Ones that come to you by referral from an existing client (these have been prescreened by your client).

• Ones that call you well in advance of their holiday.

• Return clients. The ones that you saw years ago and they have a new pet.

# The Home Visit and Types of Clients

The central duties you will be asked to do as a pet sitter are:

- feeding the pet

- getting the dog out to the bathroom

- exercise, especially if this is a dog, but some cats are into this as well

Some people assume this is all you do, but you, I, and people that hire you know better. This is just a starting list. You'll end up doing much more, but what it specifically will be depends on the circumstances.

Let's start with the timings for the visits. Clients may want you to visit their home once at mid-day. Others want you several times a day. Some want you to go to the house during the week, while others need their pets cared for on the weekends. Then there are those that go on extended holidays. Let's look at each type of client.

## The Worker

This client works all day and she wants her dog let out in the middle of the day so he can go to the bathroom and get a little exercise. It could also be a cat that needs medication or special care. This allows the client to come home late and not feel guilty. This is a great client to have because she takes the hard-to-fill time in the middle of the day. Sometimes, she may suddenly find she can't get home. A late afternoon visit and feeding may be desired, so having you "on call" may be something she'll want to arrange.

## The Business Tripper

This client is often called away for a few days at a time on business. By necessity, she is away a few nights at a time, usually during the workweek. If she has a cat, you may be asked to go once or twice each day. If it's a dog, it could be two or three times, depending on the dog. She may even get you to pick up the dog, drop him off at daycare, and get him back home later.

This type of client may not be able to give you much notice and you may charge a little extra for being available. But, adding an extra charge doesn't look good from the client's perspective. Instead, we get around this by offering the client a discount for booking early and providing a deposit. It looks like you are giving the ones that book early a break rather than penalizing the ones that book you at the last minute.

In fact, advertise this discount so you can encourage people to book early. You could have two discounts—one for people that book two months in advance and another for clients that book more than two weeks ahead. They don't have to big discounts, but people pay attention to them.

## The Weekender

This client goes away overnight or for a few days at a time, but it's on a weekend. She wants someone who can take over as she leaves town and look after things until she gets back. She normally books in advance so it makes planning easier.

## The Vacationer

This client goes away for a week or two (or more) at a time, normally booking months in advance. She may not use you often, but she values your service. She also lets you plan your pet sitting schedule well in advance.

With extended absences, clients may ask you to stay in their home. We'll look at this under other services you can provide later on.

A Mix of Clients

Not every client fits into these categories. You'll find that some are a mish-mash with different needs. And, a client that traditionally calls you for mid-week lunch-time visits may suddenly want to go away for a week.

You'll probably develop a preference for which client you want to cater to, but if you want a successful business, you can't just take one type. You need a mix of the clients to fill your day.

In the morning you look after the dogs belonging to people away on holidays. Mid-day, you can tend to cats that require one daily visit and the dogs that need a lunchtime bathroom break or a walk. Later on, you go back to the dogs that need their second visit. A balance between the ones that book during the week and the ones you cater to on weekends is also needed.

But, don't fret on how to do this. Pet sitters I talk to say that it seems to just fall into place. They tend to get just right number of each client and their days fill up very well.

If you are a numbers person, you can track how much income you get from each of the different clients. If you find that one segment is demanding more of your time, you can then focus on increasing the other types. This can be done through just taking on the type of clients you want, or you can start to refuse to pet sit for some of the undesirable clients that you may have. This will eventually help balance your workload.

You may wonder what I mean by undesirable. This is the client that doesn't respect your time by calling at the last minute and demanding service. The other extreme is the one that books you and then cancels at the last minute. Many pet sitters charge a cancellation fee if the client cancels too late. This is justified because you may have turned away other potential bookings because your time was booked. This is especially important at holiday time. It's best to get a deposit and the client forfeits the deposit for cancelling out.

And, there are some clients you'd just rather not service. You'll know in your heart when these arise.

## Daily planning

For people that are away, you will likely do two visits a day. The person's location has a significant bearing on how suitable they are as a client for you. If they are far away, you have to charge more. If it's too far, they may not be able to afford your traveling costs. Finding someone that services their area may save them some money.

You may plan each visit for a half-hour to keep on schedule. But, this is only going to be the average. What you will quickly find is that visits can be longer and shorter, depending on what is going on. They may run 20 to 40 minutes for each stop. Cats tend to take less time than dogs, but there are exceptions. Homes with more than one pet take longer.

Plans can also fall apart. You might go into a home and there is Kirby, a three-year old male cat. He is slow to move and hasn't eaten. You check his litterbox and it is dry but well-trampled. It turns out he has a blockage in his urinary system. Kirby needs veterinary help right now. This means that you need to get him to the hospital and this is going to throw you off schedule. Sometimes, your entire day's plans can go off the rails and you end up getting back home two hours after you anticipated.

This is the unpredictable part of being a pet sitter. It can be stressful at times, but remember, if you need a therapy session, go and cuddle a cat or throw a ball for a dog. Your job can be therapeutic!

## Client and Pet Files Tell you What to Do

Businesses thrive on information, and even your pet sitting enterprise needs to collect data. This helps you provide the best care to your clients and their animals. I have forms available on my website. Feel free to use these and, if you want, post them on your web site for clients to download. If they fill them out before your initial interview, it will save you time.

The first form you need is a client information form. It contains essential information such as the client's name and address as well as contact numbers (home, work, and cell). You may also want to include an email address if you are planning on sending newsletters out.

This could include information on the home itself. If there is a security system, how do you operate it? If you are adding any basic home care, you want to know what day garbage pickup is, where to pick up the mail, are there timers on lights you need to adjust if there is a power outage? What plants need watering? If there is a house problem and you can't contact the owner, who are you supposed to call?

Each pet should get its own sheet (or card). This pet information form should include the pet's name, date of birth (if you celebrate pet birthdays by sending out birthday cards this is useful information), health concerns, medications he may be on, and feeding. This last point may include his feeding schedule, what he eats (type and quantity), and any special feeding tips (such as the cat likes the food on top of the dryer).

When it comes to medication, find out what it is and the dose. If it's just for a short time, when does it finish? How is the medication given, and if you have questions about it, who do you call?

Make sure you have emergency contact information. I'll be looking at this in the next lesson, but it includes the pet's veterinarian and groomer (if the dog has one).

Try and gather information on the pet's habits. Is he a cat that hides when you arrive? You might only know if he's okay by his food disappearing. Is he a social butterfly and craves attention? Is he a dog that pulls you down the sidewalk? Is he content to sit on your lap and loves attention? You want to know what's normal so that you'll recognize if a health issue is brewing.

For health purposes, what should you be looking for that can indicate a problem? What has he had in the past that may resurface?

The reason we want a separate card for each pet is that you are going to periodically add new arrivals or, unfortunately, remove a sheet because of loss of a pet, either from death or finding a new home.

Now that you are armed with information, let's go to the house. How do you get in? That's with a key, so let's delve into what you need to know about handling keys. Don't think you can just put them in your pocket and forget about them.

## Managing Keys

When the client gives you the key, ask for a backup copy or find out if they hide one outside the house. Some people arrange lockboxes that contain a key you can access. These are like the boxes real estate agents use.

By having a source for a second key, if you lose one or get locked out the house while you are in the backyard, you can get back in. An alternative is to ask the client for contact information for a close-by person who has a key in case of emergency.

You are probably going to tag your keys, but use a code that won't tell a burglar who may find the keys where the house is to clean it out.

Many houses have security systems. Confirm the alarm codes and find out who to call (which security company) if you mistakenly trigger the alarm. This means you also need security codes with the alarm monitoring company. Don't have the key tagged with the alarm code. If you need a garage door opener, get one.

When you finish the job, don't leave the key in an unsecure place like under the mat. Also, don't leave them on the kitchen counter. If the owner phones you because she is delayed, you still need access. Having the key on you can also help if the owner loses her keys.

If the client uses your services regularly, it's best if you keep the key. If the client wants it back, they can pick it up from you or you can deliver it and charge a key drop-off fee (make sure you explain this before you pet sit so they don't have a surprise).

If you are regularly storing keys at home, invest in a safe. Your clients will feel better if they know you are diligent in your key-handling.

When you arrive at the house, especially the first time, knock on the door. Sometimes, the trip may have been cancelled at the last minute or a family member (like the teenage daughter) decided to stay home. You don't want to surprise anyone.

When you go in, do a quick check for security. This is mainly for your safety, but you want to see if the house is in good order. Look at doors and windows. See if there is any evidence of someone being in the house.

Finally we are getting to the reason you are doing this line of work. Let's look at the pets.

## Pet Care

As soon as you enter a home, the dog will be demanding your attention; the cat, well, that's up to him. The first thing on a dog's mind is usually, "let me out". Next, they want to get fed. A little attention would be appreciated too. The point is that the dog should be waiting at the door. If he isn't, either he's deaf (a common problem with older dogs), he has mobility problems, or there is a health concern.

Cats just want food or attention. If they aren't the type that come to the door to greet you, you will know where to look because you've already asked where their favorite hiding places are. This way, you can check on them.

A brief list of the duties might include:

- Let dogs out (secured fenced area or on a leash with you)

- Wash pet dishes

- Scoop the litter

- Feed the pets

- Give medications as needed

- Check the house for pet accidents or anything abnormal that involves them

- Brush the dog/cat as required

- House-sitting services (mail, newspaper, lights, garbage)

- Leave with the house secure

You want to maintain the pet's routine as normal as possible. Don't forget – that's why you are going to the house in the first place. As we go through these sections, you'll probably think – we've covered it already. We have, but this is a refresher with a different slant.

Now, let's look at feeding. First, what food were you told to feed? Changing foods could cause digestive upsets, but it could be more serious than that. A cat may be on a special food to prevent bladder stones. A dog might be allergic to chicken or on a special food for his arthritis. Ask the owner what food the pet gets and write it down in the pet file. If it's a special food, ask where it can be bought, just in case you run out. Owners usually leave enough food so that you don't have to buy any, but knowing this information can be handy.

How much food do you feed? Some pets are on diets to maintain or reduce their weight and you don't want to mess up any progress that has been made. What I find is that pets often lose weight when they are with the pet sitter. This isn't due to more exercise because that normally doesn't change. If anything, they do more sleeping with no one in the house. The reason they shrink is because the pet sitter keeps to the amount and does not feed excess treats. You look good when the owner comes home to a leaner, healthier pet. Do you think this Dachshund could lose a few pounds?

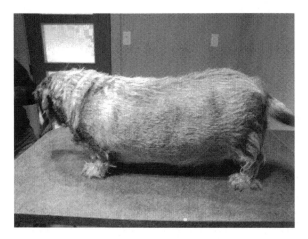

Your introductory home visit is where you find out everything you need to know about feeding. Where is the food stored? Where are the can openers, can lids, and dishes kept?

Are there are any special directions? Does the cat like the canned food piled up like a volcano? (Yes – I have a client that says her cat likes it better that way.) Should you add a little water (hot or cold?) to the dog's kibble? Do you feed the canned food first and then the dry? Is there a specific location the pet likes to be fed? Especially with cats, moving the food or water dish can upset them and stop them eating.

Multiple pets are more of a challenge. Where you put the dishes is very important, as well as the order you put the food down. I have four cats and if I get out of order or put the plates in the wrong place, they are confused and often fight. Don't let the dog eat the cat food. This is why you might have to feed the cat in a different room or in an elevated position (on the counter or dryer). Get the owner to tell you the routine so you get it right.

And, always make sure there is access to water. Put a second bowl down. If the dog drops something into a bowl and it doesn't taste good, there will be a second one to drink from. Some owners use special water. Is it the filtered water from the refrigerator? Is it bottled water? Or, is tap water sufficient?

If you have a cat and a dog, you may need a special water bowl for the cat that the dog can't reach. You don't want the dog draining the bowl or the cat going without because she won't drink the dog's water.

You may find some cats are finicky about water. Some like ice cubes put in the bowl, twice daily. Some people call this extravagant, but to pet owners, it's just what you do. If a client asks you to do these things, don't roll your eyes. Tell them you'll be glad to do it. Just tell them you do things like this every day (and you probably will).

The last thing to look at with feeding and watering is care of the bowls. You may just put them in the dishwasher or you might want to wash them so you can re-use them. Try to avoid re-using dirty bowls. The little bit of food left can have bacteria growing in it.

Now, let's look at the business side of things, poop and pee business that is.

If you are looking after cats, chances are they'll use litter boxes. While you are checking the locations of the litter boxes on your first visit, look at the litter. If it looks unfamiliar, ask the owner what type it is. It may be a brand that you can only buy at one store and you have to know where that is. Some pet sitters keep bags of common litter brands in their car just in case.

Dogs usually don't use litter boxes, but I do have some clients that have trained small dogs to pee pads. But, the majority of dogs go outside to relieve themselves. Dogs need at least two outings each day. Puppies and older dogs need more.

Dogs make your job easy. Each time you send them to the back yard, they urinate. Most defecate as well. But, some won't poop unless they are comfortable and nothing else is demanding their attention.

Think of it like this. The dog hasn't seen anyone for 12 hours. You arrive. Do you think the dog will even consider going poop unless he is really full? He'd rather have your company and won't let you out of his sight. This may mean you have to put him out in the yard, by himself for a little longer, so he eventually goes.

Some clients don't have a backyard so their dogs must be walked to eliminate. This usually becomes a combination exercise/elimination session.

Some owners have secure pens for their dogs. This means you can feed and let the dog into its pen in the morning and then feed him and put him inside at night. But, because of security (for both the house and the dog), some owners prefer to keep their dog inside the house.

## Exercise Time – Dog Walks

There's probably nothing more embarrassing than showing up at the client's home for the first time, taking the dog out, and getting lost. I had a friend take my dog Courtney on a walk and she went into some trails she was unfamiliar with. After seeing the same tree three times, she knew she was lost. She slackened the leash, put my dog ahead of her, and said "go home". Courtney brought her home.

So, before you go out with the dog on the street, get some information. If you don't know the area, get a map. This is easy to do with Google maps or you can purchase a printed copy.

Find out what type of collar the dog prefers – a harness, choke collar, or what I call "leader-type" halters. If the owner provides a leash that you think may break, use your own and satisfy yourself that the dog is secure. We double leash at my hospital. We use a collar and leash and we also loop another leash around the neck for added security.

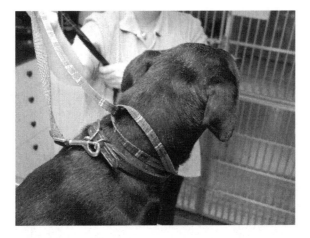

What restraint do you need? Some owners tell me their dog doesn't need a leash because he is faithful and follows you. NEVER take a dog out without a leash. He's not familiar with you and even the most trained dog isn't perfect. If the dog runs across the street and gets hit by a car, you've got a problem.

Let's look at the scenario of when a dog gets hit. Most people think the driver is to blame, but the car driver has no liability in this case. Interestingly, if a dog causes damage to a car, the car owner can sue the dog owner (or at least their insurance company does). If the dog has been entrusted to your care, guess who the insurance company comes after? You! We'll look at business insurance later.

Let's get back to the dog you were walking. If you walk in inclement weather, does the dog wear a coat? This is not important in Florida, but in the winter up north, some need protection from cold or rain, especially if they are old or have a sparse coat.

And, are treats incorporated into the walk? These could be used for training in puppies as you go along. In adult dogs, the reward should be the walk itself, not more food.

You might include two walks each day for the dog, but price your visit based on what this entails. If you are just going out the front door and block down the street, it doesn't take long. If you have to drive to a local park to walk the dog or take him to an off-leash area, it will take longer (as well as automobile costs) so you should charge more.

Does the dog get along with other dogs? And, are there any dogs along the route that you need to be wary about? Has the dog you are walking been known to bite? This last fact is important to know. If you are walking a dog that has bitten before, and more importantly, if it is recorded, if a similar instance happens, it could invalidate your insurance. Ask owners if there are any bite histories on their dogs. In some cases, you may want this included on a client form that they sign.

Let's suppose you are out with Molly the miniature Schnauzer and another dog comes along and picks a fight. How do you break them up? One way, if they are on leashes, is to simply pull the dogs apart. Do not, ever, try to pull them apart by pulling on the collars. This is how you get bitten.

If they are loose, pull the hind leg of the one you think is dominant (the aggressor). Pull fast and hard enough that you pull the dog away from the one he is biting. You want to surprise the dog so that he will break his focus and look at you. You can then tell him to sit (control him) or to go away. Just asking dogs to break it up won't work—they are in too much of a frenzy.

## Cat Exercise

Cats don't need much exercise. I prefer to say they need to be entertained. Try to provide some stimulation and exercise every day. This could just be a stalk and pounce after a feather dangling from a line at the end of a stick, or he might like to toss a furry mouse in the air or run after a table tennis ball. If you want to entertain him on a budget, try a crumpled up ball of paper, aluminum foil, the inside roll from toilet paper, or even an old cotton sock tied in a knot. One of my cats likes to play with a dripping bathtub faucet.

I have some clients that walk their cat on a leash. Cats have to be trained to do this. You can't just decide that you will take the cat out – you'll end up with a cat on its back, biting the leash. And, if you are out with a cat, be prepared to pull him up into your arms if a dog walks by. Always make sure the harness the cat wears (collars really don't control a cat well) is snug and he can't back out of it.

## Other Things you can do in the Home

If the owner is going to be away for any length of time, you will probably want to launder the dog's (and cat's) bed. Ask the owner to leave a second set of blankets/towels so you can replace them. If you want to use the owner's washing machine, ask their permission and never leave the machine running and leave the house. It is usually better for your schedule to take the laundry to the Laundromat (or your home if you can do it there). And, charge for the service if it's appropriate.

## The Parting Note

There is one thing you can do at the end of every visit that can have an extraordinary impact on what the client thinks of you. All it costs is a little time. It is leaving a note.

These notes don't have to say much. It could be as simple as "Boris was a great cat to work with (again). He was eating well and the house had no mishaps". You can also put a note about the cat noticing the squirrel outside or the dog making a new friend on his walk.

Or you could tell the client that you did something extra (took out the garbage, watered the dry plant on the windowsill) or that you thought Misty has been scratching her left ear and perhaps they want to get it checked. It doesn't take much time and you can do it while Bailey is out having a bathroom break or Sylvester is eating.

Some pet sitters keep a daily journal and leave it in the house. Also, remember I talked about having a note book? If you've been scribbling notes for the last week, put them on one page and leave it for the owners.

Writing notes may also prevent a phone call when the owners get back. They may want to know if there was any problem with the alarm system or if you noticed that Bailey was drinking more.

## Things to have in the car

- Business cards and client/pet forms

- Can opener

- Car emergency kit

- Pet restraints (leashes, pet carriers)

- Change of clothing (in case you get peed on)

- Cleaning supplies

- Stain remover

- Contact information – local SPCA, veterinarians

- Digital camera

- First aid kit (for pets and people)

- Flashlight and a second set of batteries

- Garbage bags

- List of client names and phone numbers

- Litter material

- Map

- Paper and pen

- Pet food

- Poop bags

- Rubber (or latex) gloves

- Treats and toys

- Cellular phone (likely in your pocket)

# How to Market your Pet Sitting Business

The key with marketing is to think of what attracts you to businesses. Consider a hairdresser, restaurant, or veterinarian. What marketing did they use? What turned you on and what turned you off?

There are two main ways to market (promote yourself). You can pay for advertising. Or, you can distribute materials to potential clients yourself through the free channels. It all depends on your budget. And, the marketing tools you ultimately use have to be effective; the effort and money you put into it has to generate results.

## Your Image (Slogan)

Can you summarize your business goal into one sentence? A slogan is an "ear-catching" phrase that tells prospective clients the reason your business exists. Here are a few I found perusing pet sitting web sites.

- Friendly, dependable care.

- Care for your loved ones, always.

- I take the time you can't.

- Pet sitting – the ultimate home-based business.

The last one is more for enticing people to become pet sitters then marketing to prospective clients, but I couldn't help including it. I'm sure you can come up with your own, but the goal is to portray a specific message.

## Professional Business Cards

When I say look professional, I'm not talking about combing your hair. I'm considering the entire marketing package. Let's start with business cards.

The cheapest way is to make your own cards. Most people have a computer and a printer so you can design and print your own. This is a way to save money, but do it right. I've seen poor messages printed on flimsy stock that don't impress at all. If you want to save money by printing them yourself, use card stock that feels substantial. And, always use a font (size of letter) that is easily readable.

You can also design your own but have them printed for free through one of several Internet companies that do this. Just do a search for "free business cards" and you'll be on your way.

The huge advantage of designing cards yourself is that you can make your cards very personal. You can put a picture of your favorite dog or cat on the card, something most businesses can't get away with. Having a picture of your pet can be an ice-breaker that can start conversations. You can even create two cards – one with a cat on it and the other a dog for different clients.

Putting your picture on a card really helps you bond to clients. Think of real estate agents. How many of them have their picture on their card? It works and it doesn't really cost any more.

When you choose a picture, make sure it is an animal you take care of. You may love horses and want to put a proud Arabian on the card, but if your pet sitting is limited to dogs, don't put it on. Conversely, if you only want to look after cats, don't highlight a Rottweiler.

What else should you put on a card? Because you don't have an office, you don't need an address. In fact, if you work from home, you don't want your address on it for privacy reasons. Use a post office box if you think you'll be getting mail. You certainly want a phone number. If you have a web site, put that on. And, if you want your clients to contact you by email, put that address on as well.

And, the most important thing with business cards – hand them out to everyone you meet. That is what they are for, so pass them around. If you pick people at random, about half will have a pet. If they don't, they know someone that does. You can also post the card on a bulletin board inside restaurants and cafes, at the supermarket, in libraries, and wherever else you see those boards with cards on them.

If you have a business card already, take a look at it. Does it exude a successful business? If you had someone make up your card (or plan to), they will help you choose the best paper (called "stock" in the printing world) and likely help you design the cards. This is one way to get a professional look, but it does cost money.

The rest of your communications must be just as professional. Keep this in mind as we look at newspaper ads, phone book listings, websites, as well as brochures.

# Brochures

The business card is designed as a contact piece—to help clients get hold of you. But, let's suppose you are marketing to people unfamiliar with pet sitters. Hiring a pet sitter is something new to them, so your job is to educate. A brochure can do this because it is a detail piece about your business.

One pet sitter I know that has an interesting brochure. It shows that she only looks after cats (she loves cats), but it also mentions the house care that she can provide. She will get the newspaper, retrieve the mail from the mail box, and even close curtains at night. She states her goal "I want to make it look like people are still in your home". Do you think she gets clients this way? You bet she does.

The easiest brochure to design and print, and the most common one used, is on an 8.5x11 sheet of paper, folded into three (what is called a tri-fold) so it has six panels. These can contain lots of information about you and your business. One panel could be a larger, more detailed version of your business card.

On another "panel", you can include a biography—why you started the business. This is your chance to show your love of animals, and yes, it can get personal with "squishy" material. Animals should be prominent because that's what you are all about. Include pictures of your pets. If you don't have any, ask your friends, relatives, and even clients if you can use a picture of their pets. Most will be glad to help you out.

And, definitely list your services so they know what you can provide. This helps the naïve client know what to ask about.

The brochure can also be your way to differentiate yourself from other pet sitting businesses, assuming you are facing competition.

List your credentials (any training that helps you do the job) and experience that could be an asset. If you completed my course, make sure you mention it. And, also point out what organizations you belong to.

What can you do with brochures? One is to drop them off at the local chamber of commerce. Leave a stack at veterinary offices, groomers, and any pet feed stores. This marketing will not generate instantaneous business; it is designed to create an interest in your services. Someone may ask their veterinarian if they know any pet sitters. The veterinarian will pass the client to the receptionist who will say "Yes, I just got a brochure from one who seems really nice." It will be yours.

Very similar to a brochure is a flyer. Think of the ones you see on bulletin boards with the little tear-off strips at the bottom. The best way to get an idea of how to design one is to go looking at others and see what gets your attention. Make the strips at the bottom large enough to include your phone number, your name, and the words "pet sitter". And, if you put one up, go around periodically and replace it so it looks fresh and you can "restock" the strips.

## Press Releases

Press releases can lead to free publicity. These are short information pieces that entice editors to ask a reporter to create an article on the topic. Papers love pet-related stories because their readers appreciate them. So, how can you do this? You need to make it easy for the paper (or magazine if there is a local one you can go to).

My exposure to this is through my writing. I author many articles every year for dog magazines. Sometimes, the editor comes to me with a press release that someone has sent her. To write the article and interview the person, I want some facts that I can build a story on as well as contact information that leads me to the interviewee. You, as a pet sitter, need to write a press release that gives the reporter all the information she needs to write a story. The easier and more interesting it is, the better chance you have of triggering a story.

Suppose you are just opening your business. You'd want to start out with:

Susan has seen her share of pet emergencies. On a recent pet sitting assignment, she was looking after Henry, a cat that couldn't pass urine. But, as she was tending to that, she was faced with another problem. The water level was rising in the basement.

This short segment is called the grab – it grabs readers' attention, and that of the editor as well.

Next, flesh out the story. In both these situations, you can emphasize the value of hiring a pet sitter. You got the cat to the veterinarian for a urinary blockage and you called the plumber to solve the burst pipe. You prevented a cat's death and saved the house from total flooding.

Once you have the press release prepared (which includes your contact information so they can interview you), send it to the paper. Don't just email it to the general mailbox. Get the email address for the managing editor, the lifestyles editor (pet stories get put in that section), and the business editor. And, always include a professionally-made photo of yourself so they know they don't have to get one taken.

Other reasons to send out press releases include expanding your services, new trends in pet sitting, and if you've made a charitable donation or sponsored an event.

Once your company is going, continue to shower the paper with press releases. These have to be topical and timely. Here are some ideas:

• Before flea season gets in full gear, write an article on flea control. People will see you as an expert. Just make sure you do your homework – perhaps talk to several veterinary offices on what they recommend.

• Heartworm. If you have a season beginning in (for example) May, get a note out about it in March (lots of lead time).

• If a pet-related issue comes to your attention, capitalize on it. If your state is considering legislation for all antifreeze to have a bittering agent to prevent pet poisoning, tell the public what a great idea that is.

• You can try one that tells a little more about you. If it's September, tell a story about the people that couldn't get a pet sitter last Christmas (and that you are taking bookings now).

The idea on these articles is that it does not give you direct advertising, but it gets your name out there as someone who cares about and has knowledge about animals. Press releases should be less than 500 words and well written. If you can't write, see if any of your clients can help you write and then offer to trade services to keep your cost down.

## Paid advertising

Most pet sitters do not pay for advertising. This is because they focus on free advertising. But, there is one thing you may want to consider – a listing in the yellow pages. It's considered the most valuable and effective way to spend your advertising dollars. This may be included in your phone cost. Don't get too fancy with this. Just get a line ad and leave the display ads for the businesses with more money.

I'm not an advocate of paying for advertising, but I will mention what you can do if you want to delve into this arena. The local paper will be glad to sell you a business card-sized ad. Depending on the size of the paper and distribution, these can be cheap or costly. If you want to do this, perhaps consider it for just a few months while you are getting started. You certainly don't need to continue if you are busy. If there is a newsletter distributed by the local shelter, see if you can include an ad in it.

Another idea is targeted marketing where you send information out to a specific area (such as a planned community). This could be through a newsletter or delivered door to door. This is usually not that expensive, but survey the market closely. It can end up with the piece being sent to people that do not have pets.

You can also buy mailing lists, but the economics of this are questionable for your type of business. It's geared more to services that can be used immediately (like carpet cleaning) and combined with a discount.

Here's an exception. In some areas, dogs are required to be licensed. And, some cities or municipalities will sell you the licensing information on these pets. When you think of it, these are perfect customers. They own a dog and they show responsibility by getting their dog licensed. In some areas, licensing requires an up-to-date rabies vaccination so these people are the cream of the crop for you to attract to your business.

Direct mail is a way to send a card or brochure to certain people. This can be advantageous if sent to past clients but postage is expensive. These people know who you are but just need a reminder to use your services.

## Vehicle Signs – The Debate

Should you invest in a vehicle sign? This is debatable. Though it will give you advertising as you drive around, your clients may not appreciate it. Think of it this way. You pull into the drive and anyone seeing you there then knows that the owners are away. You could be setting the house up for a burglary.

In fact, some pet sitting companies want the clients' absence to not be detectable. So, you enter the home like you belong, don't wear a uniform, and don't mark your car with any advertising.

## Joining Groups and Speaking engagements

You can join as many groups are you want, but only join those that will help you gain more business. These include the Chamber of Commerce, pet sitters' organizations, and the SPCA. Before you join, ask what will it do for you?

For example, the Chamber is a good source of referrals because the people that belong will either have pets themselves, or they know a large number of people (they tend to be the networking type) they can tell about you. But, if the Chamber doesn't include many people from the area you are servicing, it's not going to help that much. The best way to evaluate it is to go and see who is there, and if they pass your test, then join.

The Better Business Bureau (BBB) is a watchdog organization for consumers. They register complaints against organizations and track how the complaints are resolved. Becoming a member can be advertised on your cards and brochures, and some consumers think that if you belong to this group, you are the one to hire.

The SPCA often has regular meetings and it can help you meet like-minded people. They may even be able to promote your services.

The pet sitters groups, such as Pet Sitters International and the National Association of Professional Pet Sitters, can be valuable to join. The most practical aspect is that they can help you get insurance, usually at lower rates that you can get by yourself. We'll talk about this later. As well, some have informative articles on how to run your pet sitting business and opportunities for advertising.

This is the point. You can join as many groups as you want, but make sure there is a reason to do so. Each one has to provide service to you. And, if you do belong to any groups, make sure they are prominently displayed on your web site or printed materials.

Do you have a knack for speaking to groups? If you can give a seminar on pet care (such as how to pet-proof their home), you have a great way of marketing yourself. It boosts your credibility and you'll be talking to people that own pets. If you are doing a talk, generate a press release about it. Potential groups are those at a shelter, a dog-walking group, and the Chamber of Commerce (you can tell them how successful your business has become).

# Phone Calls

When someone calls to ask about your services, the only question they will likely ask is – "how much do you charge to look after my dog Scruffy?" They do this because they don't know what else to ask. They are not aware of all the things you do.

There are two ways you can handle this question. One is to simply answer it and say "I charge $25 a day for pet sitting services." The client will go away with the thought that she can phone another pet sitter and, if they charge a dollar less, book with them and get the same services.

You know, and I know, you are providing a better service, but the customer doesn't know this. This is how I would control the conversation for maximum benefit to me as a pet sitter. I've included the rationale for each question I ask.

Client: I'm calling about your pet sitting service. How much do you charge?

Me: I'd love to answer that question, but let's find out what you need. Can you tell me if you have a cat or dog? (You probably have different rates for different species.)

Client: I have a dog.

Me: And, what breed of dog is it and what's her name? (People like to talk about their pets. You can then see if you should offer walking services if it's a large dog.)

Client: I have a Shih Tzu named Molly.

Me: And how old is she? (From now on I refer to the dog as she or Molly, and I want to know if she is senior pet or not.)

Client: She is 12 years old.

Me: I can see why you might want a pet sitter to keep Molly in her home while you are away. How long are you going to be away? (You have said something that the client will agree with and you are empathizing with her thoughts (bonding with her) and now you look at what the client wants for pet sitting services.)

Client: I'm planning on two trips, but the first one is just overnight, but I'll be away from early one morning to late the next night.

Me: I normally do two visits a day, but I can do more. Will this be enough for Molly or does she need to get out more often than that? (This shows I care for Molly and we'll create a visitation schedule that the dog can cope with.)

Client: I usually walk Molly twice each day and she goes out several times in the backyard between those times.

Me: I would recommend three visits a day for Molly, and I can certainly give her a walk in the morning and the evening visit. (Now I know Molly's needs.)

This conversation would go on to where I tell the caller exactly what I do when I visit and then, after all the talking, I would introduce the cost of providing the service. Can you see how much more effective this would be in educating the client about what you do? It also starts to create a bond between you. She can't help but say "Yes, are you available the second weekend in October?"

If the client books you, or even if she doesn't, offer to send some material to her (by post or email) so that your name can stay in her mind. This packet can include a price list. You might want to include an information sheet on how to choose a pet sitter, of course, geared to show that yours is the one she should select.

Here's an experience I had with a bed and breakfast. I sent them an email about availability in the summer and they sent a nice note telling me they were already booked. I didn't hear from them until the next New Year. They sent me a greeting, pictures of their place at Christmas, and another note hoping they could accommodate me in the next year. And yes, I will consider them. These follow-up emails are valuable yet cost nothing.

Put this idea into the pet sitting world. If you have email addresses, think of a package you can send out to people that asked for information. It may only take a reminder like this to get a booking.

## Neat Things to do with your Clients

Here is a plethora of ideas on what you can do to enhance your business. You can't do them all, but you may find one or two that you think make sense for you.

Using the Camera

While you are looking after the pet, take a photo and email it to the owners while they are away. Most people are on email these days, so this is simple. Don't send a long note by email unless you want a long note back that you may feel compelled to reply to. This can be a big time-waster. Just say something like "Lady says she misses you, but is enjoying her walks with me." I'm sure you can dream up something the dog or cat would say.

If you have a small photo printer, take a picture of the pet when the owner is away and leave it for their return so they can see how relaxed their friend was.

As well, you can print a photo and put it in the file. This serves two purposes – one is that you have a ready reminder of the pet. The other is that you have a photo if the pet gets lost.

Death of a Pet

What should you do when a client loses a loved pet? This is what I do. I send a card expressing my sympathies. If I know the client and the pet really well, I may send some flowers or a plant. What you do will be up to you; it depends what you are comfortable doing.

## A Check-off Sheet

Create a check-off sheet that lists the services you offer. Some of these you'll likely offer for free, such as picking up the newspapers or putting out the garbage. Even though you would normally provide this care, include them on the list so the client knows you do it.

You can also include other tasks you want to charge for, such as nail trimming, grooming, longer walks for the dog, plant watering, collecting mail, taking the pet to the groomer or veterinarian, and increasing your daily visits from two to three. Then, there is house stuff such as being there to let a furnace man in or other "home" appointments.

# Distributing Material

You can also distribute your material at places people go for other pet services. In this case, think of veterinarians, groomers, pet stores, feed stores, and even shops like pet bakeries. I would not approach kennels because you are competing with them. However, if you are providing a dog walking service, you could tell them about that.

Another source for client contacts is your answering machine. Ask for a mailing address (or an email address) so you can follow up with more than just a return phone call.

Next, we move into the electronic age, and the opportunities in that arena are almost endless, and changing each year.

## Your Web Site

In this day and age, a web site seems to be a must. In fact, some people may decide not to do business with you if you don't have one. But, the first thing you want to do is figure out if you need one, and if you do, what is its function? The time you don't need one is when you are already busy and your other marketing efforts are doing their job.

If you decide that you want one, I would keep it small so that you are not spending lots in both time and money maintaining it. The information that is essential is:

• Contact information

• Your biography (written so the reader thinks you are the best pet sitter available)

• Business facts (how long you've been around, what areas you service)

• A listing of services and what animals you will sit, as well as examples of fees

• You can, of course, add much more. Here's some ideas:

• Information pieces that are relevant to your business

• Highlight products you sell

• List of other businesses that refer to you (this will keep them referring)

• A gallery of pets you look after

• Testimonials from clients

• An FAQ section, answering questions that routinely come up in the initial consultation (registration forms can also be included.)

You can generate a website yourself by learning how to do it. You can also hire someone, but unless this is your brother, it can get expensive. If you are putting up a site, make sure it is always updated. The simpler it is, the better. The more complicated it is, the more often you need to work on it.

If you have a website, put the address on all business forms, cards, and brochures. Tell all clients you speak to that they can get information on you (and your staff) by visiting the site. Put the address on your phone answering message.

## Newsletters

Another way to use computers is to send out a regular newsletter. I do this at my hospital. I send it out to about 1000 clients every month, and it contains information on what the hospital is doing, topical advice (when to start flea preventives and such), as well as the popular features – a pet photo and the joke. You can also remind clients to book your services early for their holidays. If you have a web site, mention it.

Newsletters can go to all clients (and even non-clients) that supply you with an email address. If you are sending out a newsletter, make sure you "blind copy" the recipients. You don't want your clients seeing other's addresses. The other way is to use one of the free services to distribute newsletters.

## Social Media

Social media is the new kid on the block. It is the new way people obtain information. Highly connected people gather information from websites but they also comment on it. This information is "published" on such forums as Facebook, Twitter, and YouTube.

You may think this is unimportant, but 91 percent of all Internet users base their buying decisions on customers' reviews. And, 87 percent trust a friend's recommendation over that of a critic—they trust their peers more than advertising.

Social media can be called a relationship building tool. If you continue to connect with people, showing your passion for your job and animals, you build an audience uniquely interested in your business. The advantage is that you can talk directly to these people rather than being filtered by editors of publications. But, here's the true power of this marketing. Rather than just talking to clients for brief periods on the phone or at their homes, you can be in contact 365 days a year.

How can you dive into this realm? First, you need a website. Everything you do on the Internet will point people back to it. Most people will visit a website before calling you. This is the foundation for talking to people.

Facebook, founded in 2004, is the most popular social network. It is friendly, social, and informal. Start by creating a personal profile and then build one for your business. Use Facebook to say things of interest to your clients and potential clients. This could be photos of neat pets you have sat, announce any talks you are giving, and you can even offer opinions on pet-related news events.

Blogs are web logs, or columns on the Internet. You need to commit time to it and keep it fresh with new information or else people won't read it. But, it can be a powerful tool in influencing people. Of course, use it to drive website traffic. You can link to interesting sites, promote yourself, and educate clients.

Twitter is a "microblog". Each entry, or tweet, is a maximum of 140 characters, which is a sentence or two. To make this work, you follow a person on Twitter. With it being a mobile-based application, the users tend to be younger. If you can understand this system, experts agree that it can be used to generate traffic on your website.

The key with these sites is that a full understanding of how they work is not needed to begin using them. Find the sites, jump in and experiment. But, don't try to do them all. Concentrate on one and do it well. You can be seen as leader that way.

## How to Get New Clients

To know the most effective ways to get more clients, you have to know who you are trying to attract. Here are two extremes. If you want to attract young, single people (this probably wouldn't be your market because they don't own pets that often), you'd probably lean towards "high-tech" advertising through the Internet. On the other hand, if you were targeting seniors, you'd want to offer brochures (less high-tech).

Knowing who your model client is can also help you decide if working with a group makes sense. If you want to donate a weekend of pet sitting to a local not-for-profit group, ask who belongs to the organization. You can imagine the difference between a group of Rotarians (a good market, by the way) and a support group for people with allergies (the majority are not likely to have pets).

From my experience, the best way to get new clients, and more of them, is through word of mouth. This can begin through your co-workers (assuming you are employed), as well as friends and family. Give them cards and brochures to show you are serious and ask them to give them to their friends that have pets.

The other word of mouth is through your existing clients. The advantage is that these people know what you can do and can tell others how well you did it. So, when you give your client a bill, include marketing materials and say that you are looking to expand your client base. Otherwise, your clients will assume you are too busy and they don't even think to tell others about you. You will also find that these people will prescreen clients for you. They don't generally say you are available if they think the prospect is a poor client for you. If you want to promote these referrals, offer a discount on the referrer's next booking.

# How to Set up a Business

You need a headquarters! You can't run a business from your car, so you need to claim some space. This could be a corner of the living room or a spare bedroom, but make it a place that won't be disturbed. You don't want to have to clean it up each time company arrives. If possible, you also want to be able to get away from the sounds of kids taunting each other or the dog barking.

At a minimum, you need room for a desk, computer, printer, a chair, and a telephone (unless you use a cell phone). A filing cabinet is useful once your client files grow, and you want to store (and later find) important papers like client files and accounting records. Then there are all the little things that make the office yours—your coffee mug, a poster for inspiration, and a picture of your favorite pet.

But, besides the home office, you will likely work out of your car as well. You can set this up in the trunk or in the back of your car (as long as it is secure). Start with a file holder so you can have your clients' files on hand. This is usually just the active files for clients you are providing services to at that time. You will also want a copy of your forms and regular stationery equipment (stapler, post-it notes, paper clips, pens).

# Types of Business Ownership

There are many different ways to structure your business. Each one has its advantages and disadvantages, so you have to decide which one is appropriate for you. To decide that, we first have to look at what the possibilities are.

Most pet sitters are sole proprietors. You are the owner, you make all the decisions, and you get all the revenue. However, there is a downside. You are also the one that risks your investment and possibly your personal assets if the business is not successful or if there is a legal issue (I'll come to that later).

A partnership is a situation where you and one or more other person(s) are the owners of the business. This also means that both of you are the managers. This helps because one partner can cover when the other goes away or has an illness. It also spreads the financial risks (good) and profits (not so good) between the two of you. If you are looking at a partnership, consider it akin to a marriage between you. If you can't get along and agree on the company philosophy—what your goals and expectations are—you shouldn't be together.

A limited partnership is a situation where you are the main owner/manager while your partner(s) is a silent investor. You do most of the managing while your partner shares the financial risk as well as the profits. One hurdle to overcome in this arrangement is deciding what salary you take for doing the work, and what proportion of the money you allocate to profits (for equal sharing).

Corporations are appealing because they remove the risk from you personally. It is expensive to set up, but in some circumstances it makes sense. In this case, each person owns shares in the corporation. To set up this up, get legal advice.

I keep talking about financial risk. I know this won't happen to you, but suppose for a moment that you own a car (with monthly payments) and you've also racked up a lot in credit card debt, all in the name of the business. If you can't manage the payments, the creditors can come after you to get their money. They could take your car, savings, or anything they can convert to cash. If there is money owed, or there is a legal case against you, setting up a corporation makes sense. It acts as a shield for your personal assets against creditors.

The other way to get into the pet sitting business is through a franchise. You, in effect, buy a license to open a "branch" of the pet sitting company in your area. A big benefit is that you get immediate recognition, assuming that the company has been advertising and people have heard of it. Franchise organizations often provide training, marketing materials, forms, and maybe even start-up loans.

The downside is that franchises expect you to follow their business plan. They may have strict guidelines on how you can advertise, what other services you can offer, and what you are permitted to sell. They often restrict you to a certain geographic area. This makes sense for them as they may want to sell another franchise in an adjoining area.

Though franchises allow you to get started quickly, there are negatives. The cost of purchasing a franchise may cost several thousand dollars. They may also expect you to contribute funds for advertising. Some even have ongoing charges where you have to pay a percentage of your sales to the parent franchise. A franchise does not guarantee a successful business—you still have to work hard to be successful.

If you are considering a franchise, do your homework. Find out if the company has ever had bankruptcy proceedings and see if there are any complaints (you can check this through a Better Business Bureau but another way is to do a search of the company on the Internet) and see what people have to say about it.

## Licensing

Check with the local zoning office to see what business you can have at home. Because you aren't going to have signage outside your home and clients aren't going to be dropping by, chances are you don't need special zoning. You can ask the clerk at the town hall or the chair of the planning board for this information.

Assuming you are clear, the next step is a business license. This allows you to have a business in the town, city, or wherever you live. This is usually less than $100 but in some places, can cost upwards of $300 and it needs renewing annually.

Some places have additional bylaws in place that require you to purchase a commercial dog walker license.

## Contracts with Customers

Many pet sitters never create a contract with their customers and do each pet sitting gig on a handshake agreement. However, contracts do have their benefits. They detail exactly what services you will provide and when, what you are going to charge for the service, and when payment is expected. It also mentions what falls as the responsibility of the client.

There are some other things that can be included.

• What do you do if a pet needs the care of a veterinarian?

• Who authorizes the pet's care?

• What financial limits (if any) does the client have on care?

• If a pet happens to die while under your care, what should be done? This could involve a post mortem, cremation, or burial.

• Include a statement that the client signs that confirms that a dog has no history of biting another dog or people.

• You may want to include a statement that the client signs that the pets are up to date on their rabies vaccination (important if it is required in your area).

• The client acknowledges that they have given you a key to their home.

• Describe what insurance you have in place and if you are bonded.

A contract is best designed by a lawyer, but I have provided a simple example. You can find it on my website.

## Business Insurance

Insurance protects you if things go wrong. You see, if you make a mistake and cause harm to property or an animal, and someone sues you and wins, they can take your assets like your car and home, as well as your savings. Insurance protects against this.

Liability insurance protects you from mishaps while you are working. Suppose you back your car in the drive and break the garage door or you leave a tap on and flood the kitchen. What if an animal dies under your care and the owner thinks you are negligent? The last one is maybe a dog under your control bites someone - the liability with the most exposure (risk of happening).

Here is a typical example. A dog that you've been walking for a year, which has never shown aggression and seems to get along with kids, decides out of the blue to bite a child. However, the bite happens to be on a little girl's face and it disfigures her. You can bet there will be someone suing you.

Even if you are not liable, just the lawyer bills alone can get costly. Insurance covers this.

If the mishap happened in your home, chances are your home insurance will cover a small business like yours (but check that if you plan to do pet sitting from your home). In most cases, you'll want your own pet sitting liability insurance to cover you. Policies can be found by talking to insurance dealers. Get several quotes to see which is the most economical and what it includes. You may get a better deal if you belong to a pet sitter organization - they have group insurance for people who do pet sitting and they often offer discounted rates.

## Bonding

Some clients will ask if you are bonded. This is a confusing issue, and once you see what bonding does, you'll understand why most pet sitters don't do get it. Let's see why.

Just to be clear, bonding does nothing to protect the client, though many clients think it does. Clients think that being bonded can help them because they're used to performance bonds. These bonds, usually taken out by construction contractors, reimburse the client if the contractor fails to perform the job the client hired them for. In these cases, the bonding company immediately pays any damages, but the contractor reimburses the bonding company.

In your situation, we're talking about bonding pet sitting employees—your employees. A bond guarantees a payment for damages in the event an employee covered by the bond causes you financial loss. This would normally be theft of your equipment or damage to your company's possessions.

Here's how it works: If you have an employee who steals (from you), you file a claim with the bonding company. The employee must be arrested, convicted, and sentenced for you to recover costs from the bonding company.

If you explain this to a client, the client can see there's no point to it.

If you're a sole proprietor, you can't bond yourself. You aren't going to do dishonest acts against your own company. You may find a bonding company through the pet sitter organizations I've mentioned or on the Internet. The cost for five employees is normally less than $100 for a $5,000 bond.

Now that you know this, is there any point to having your employees bonded? Well, most bonding companies do background checks on the employees you want bonded. You can also do background checks independently, and that approach could be cheaper. Making background checks (through a bonding company or independently) will show your clients that you're doing due diligence and hiring only reputable employees.

Now let's look at the client side. Let's suppose a client claims your employee stole from him or her. The client calls the police to have it investigated, and the police create a report. Next, the client calls his or her insurance company and reports a theft. The insurance company pays the client for the loss, minus the deductible. The client is only out the cost of the deductible, so it normally ends there.

## Personal Insurance

In my younger days, if an insurance person came to talk to me, my eyes would glaze over and my ears wouldn't seem to work. I just wasn't interested. But, as your life changes, it takes on an importance of its own. There are many types of personal insurance; what type is required depends on your situation.

Life insurance isn't for you; it's for the people you leave behind. Are you going to saddle others with debt if you die? Talk to your loved ones and find out if they can survive (financially) without you. If they can't, talk to an insurance salesman about how much coverage is appropriate and the costs of such a policy.

Another insurance you may want to consider is disability insurance. Disability insurance provides coverage if you are injured (any cause) and cannot perform your work. If your income is not required to keep the household going, then it is unnecessary. On the other hand, if your income is essential, you may want to look at a policy. If are worried, talk to your insurance agent. The main argument against disability insurance is the cost. It is expensive.

Finally, health insurance. How much this costs depends on where you live. In Canada where I am, the cost is relatively low for a single person. However, in other places (I'm thinking the US here), it can be very expensive. Insurance like this is designed to even out the costs. When looking at this type of insurance, some cover medical, dental, chiropractors, and even eyeglasses.

Some of you have a working spouse that can extend his/her health insurance benefits to you. If that is the case, great. But, if you don't have insurance, who is going to pay a large hospital bill if you get sick? Make sure you have coverage so that an illness won't bankrupt you. I consider health insurance a necessity.

And, let's move to your car for a moment. Check your policy to make sure it covers you using it for business. You may need a commercial policy to use it for a pet sitting business. Here are some things to look into:

- Does it cover pets you are transporting?

- Do you need business signage or not?

I know insurance can be daunting. It is something that you will learn about as you go forward with your business. The main thing I want you to do is - be prepared. Don't put off getting insurance until the day that an accident occurs and then wish you had it.

## Your Business Hours

One thing we've alluded to, but really haven't talked about, is your hours. The good news is that it's your business and you get to set whatever hours you want. This is how my wife (she is a veterinarian as well) and I work. I am the early morning guy. I get up at 6 am because I want to. This gives me time to do some writing or exercise before my day gets going. I arrive promptly at the office for 8:30, usually before, to see my patients. On the other hand, my wife is slower to get up. Rising at 6 am is punishment to her. So, what have we done to accommodate this? Louise starts works a little later.

But there is another factor to consider—your clients' desires. Your clients will, in the end, determine when you work. Pet sitting does not often conform to a 9 to 5 schedule. If your business is typical, you will find that the busy times are morning, midday, and late afternoon/early evening. A generalization is that you will look after the pets early and late and take dogs for walks in the middle.

The hardest thing to do is draw a line between your business and personal lives. If you let people call and you answer the phone at 9:00 p.m., they'll come to expect it. Here's a simple first step you can take—have two phones, one for the business calls and one for personal use. This allows you to shut off the business phone at a predetermined time and take the evening off.

Another thing I encourage you to do is to be realistic about how many hours you can work. If you work too hard, you may suffer from burnout. This does not happen immediately. It happens when you are successful and business is great. You've been working 12 hours (or more) every day and you've been doing it for over a year. You just can't keep it up.

Hard work is appropriate in some cases. For example, if you are preparing to expand the business to justify an employee. However, if you plan to keep working until you retire, limit your hours so you can keep going for years.

## When to Hire Help

Hiring staff is a big step. It's a decision you must look at carefully and you need to examine all the reasons why you may want (or not want) to do it.

Employees can take the strain off you and help your business run better. They allow you to take on more clients and provide better service because you have more work hours available. Especially important is your enhanced ability to cover holiday weekends. You can look after more pets, and at the same time, create more income.

You can either hire staff as soon as you start up, or you can wait until you grow to where there is too much work for you. There is no right or wrong way to do this; what it comes down to is your ability to pay an employee; or more specifically, can your income take a hit?

Consider this. The first person to get paid is the employee. As the boss, you come second (or third if you have two employees). Can you afford to not get paid, or have a reduced income while the work load is building?

But, besides the monetary cost, employees can be a burden in other ways, especially if you don't hire the right one. And this is the biggest challenge with employees—hiring the best person possible.

What do I look for in an employee? I want them to be a people person, reliable, and dedicated. If you have 15 houses to visit in a day as well as two appointments with prospective clients, you depend on your employee. If s/he does not turn up, you have a problem. It can be difficult to find the right person, but it is worth the effort, and sometimes, the wait.

You can find great candidates by considering students, retirees, and at-home homemakers. You can find these people by asking at pet shelters (talk to the people who volunteer to walk dogs at the local shelter), dog parks, and even local dog clubs or 4H groups.

Background checks are essential when hiring employees. Don't forget – you are going to give them access to your clients' homes and they are usually working without supervision.

You also want to ensure employees are adequately trained so that they can provide the same level of service that your clients have come to expect from you. A procedures manual describing how to do the job can help them understand what you want done and how you want it done.

The other thing you have to decide is, are you going to hire an employee part-time or full-time? Ultimately, it depends on how much work you want to pass on to another person. If you can get someone part-time who is flexible, that is the best possible solution for you.

An alternative to an employee is a partner. This means you share the business with another person. Both of you contribute funds and energy to the business. Both of you have to possess the same goals and work ethics. This can be a great arrangement when you want to take a little time off because both of you take responsibility for the business. Of course, you only get to take home half the profits.

But, partnerships can be a problem if a disagreement starts. A partnership is like a marriage. If you are contemplating a union with another person, it may be a good idea to have a partnership agreement drawn up by a lawyer. It won't prevent a break-up, but it can make a separation smoother. It also details what responsibilities each of you have in the partnership. I know an agreement saved me when I wanted to leave a veterinary hospital by exiting the partnership. It made it much simpler. I've talked to ex-partners who had a battle akin to a divorce between them.

But, here's another idea for you. If you can strike up a relationship with another pet sitter, you can help each other. For example, if you are planning on being away, perhaps s/he can take your clients. And, you can reciprocate and provide the same service for them if they are away or sick. The key with this, again, is being reliable and professional (don't try to take customers from the competition).

## The Cost of Employees

When considering hiring a new employee, ask yourself these questions. Will it make my day easier with someone else sharing the work load? Will it make me more profit?

If hiring an employee doesn't do at least one of these, there is no point in hiring one. If it does both, then hiring another person makes sense.

Do a financial analysis on what the new employee will do for you. Look at all the expenses of the new hire. Next, look at the positives. If it will increase the amount of revenue you can generate by taking on new customers, that's good. If you can cut your day from 14 hours to a manageable 10, that's also good.

You know this, but I'll stress it once more. Employees cost money. In fact, there are lots of expenses you probably never thought about when hiring an employee. This includes the wages, contributions to social security, workers' compensation, and unemployment taxes/contributions.

Workers' Compensation covers employees for injuries that occur when they are performing their job responsibilities. More information on this program is available from the government agency that administers the program.

You are also required to withhold taxes and unemployment contributions (employment insurance in Canada). All of this can be organized by your accountant or knowledgeable bookkeeper, but you can manage it once you know how.

And, while you don't get paid for taking a holiday, they do. And, they get paid for statutory holidays while you don't. That's what you are getting yourself into as an employer.

## Your Safety

Let's finish off our employee talk with as little about safety – both for you and for your staff. Chances are, you are going to get the occasional cat scratch or a dog bite, but you want to minimize them as much as possible.

Know the pets you are looking after. Ask the owner if their pet is aggressive or has bitten or hurt anyone. If they have, put a note in the pet's file to remind you. Ask what sets the pet off and how you can prevent it. If there are issues, use muzzles and other restraint devices.

There is also the issue of diseases that are transmissible from pet to person, what we call zoonoses. The most obvious one is rabies. This viral disease can kill you if you are infected by a dog or cat bite. This is why most pet sitters ask for a current rabies vaccination certificate.

With cats, we can contract cat scratch fever. Because it is transmitted in flea feces and "injected" into you with a cat scratch, if the cats you look after are on flea control, there is little chance of being infected with this bacterium. But, common sense says that if you get a bad scratch or bite see your doctor.

Diarrhea in dogs is sometimes due to organisms that can also infect you. Giardia (also known as beaver fever) is one example. If you are caring for a dog that has diarrhea, wash your hands well to prevent transmission.

There is also a fairly benign disease you can catch called ringworm, though there is a strong social stigma surrounding this fungal infection. Chances are, you'll pick this up from a kitten with areas of hair loss on its body.

Another hazard is allergies to cats and dogs. These are common, but I'm sure you wouldn't be pursuing this career if you suffered from this malady.

## Start-up Costs

What start-up expenses will you have? There are two major expenses you need to spend money on before you go to your first pet sitting assignment. One is a car. It must be reliable and obviously not too old. Picture you going on your first "interview" with a client and your transportation is a rusty, smoke-billowing truck. Do you think the client is going to have faith that you will make it to their home when you need to get there? You need a car that exudes confidence – confidence that you will be able to get to their home twice each day.

You also don't want it to be too clean and pristine. Show them that you are willing to put dogs in your car so that you can take them to the park for a romp.

If you are looking for cars, it would be wonderful to buy new, but you may not be able to afford that. More likely, you will settle for a car a few years old with modest miles. Buy one that is easy on gas so that visits to the gas station won't eat up your profits.

The other expense is marketing and advertising. You can produce many marketing materials on your home computer with a basic printer. In that case, you need to invest more time than money, but even paper and ink does not grow on trees.

Borrowing is likely going to be something you need to look at. You can't start a business without money. There is a simple guideline – borrow as little as you can, but as much as you need.

There are two kinds of money you need to carry on your pet sitting business. One is start-up money. This is the amount you need to get the business running. This pays for all the start-up expenses and in many cases, is less than $5000.

However, there are ways to cut costs. If you start part-time and continue working until pet sitting gets busy enough to fund itself, you can fund it as you go. This way, you won't have to get a bank loan.

## Accounting—Day-to-Day Money Management

The two important things accounting tells you are what your income is and what your expenses are. If you don't know this, you could wake up one day and suddenly be out of money.

One way to make this job easier is to take a class in accounting. Make sure it is designed for small business. You don't want to learn accounting for managing a multi-million dollar company.

When you initially set up your business, the first thing you'll want to do is establish your fiscal year. This is when your financial year begins and ends. Most people choose the calendar year, beginning January 1st and ending December 31st. This coincides with your personal tax year which makes things a lot simpler.

Corporations often have a different tax year for business reasons, and they don't align with the calendar year. Your accountant can give you advice on this.

The next thing to do is set up a way to track expenses. Start by keeping every receipt for every penny you spend on business expenses. One way to track these is with a checkbook. Get an account for your business and keep it separate from your personal banking. At first you may want to just open another personal account devoted to the business. The reason is that account fees for personal accounts tend to be lower than those for business. Another way to keep a listing of expenses is to run everything through a credit card.

The biggest expense you are going to have is your car. This is because you have to travel from client to client, sometimes several times each day. But, sometimes it is the same car you use personally. There are two ways you can manage these auto expenses.

One is to record every expense you have such as gas, oil changes, tires, etc. You then figure out what mileage is done by the business and how much you do personally. This means keeping a log of the odometer every time you take the car out. The portion of mileage attributed to the business means that share of the car expenses is a business expense.

Another way involves tallying the mileage, but instead of keeping receipts, you use the mileage rate calculated by the government. If you have a newer car that is economical to run, this may be an advantage for you. The rate changes annually, so make sure you use a current number.

You also need to track income. This could be a listing of each deposit you make into your account (as long as you just take cash and checks) or a total of all the receipts. Do these totals at least monthly and reconcile it with your account statement.

If you like writing numbers down, you can use a ledger notebook to track expenses. You set up one column for income (unless you want to break the income down into categories such as different types of pet sitting and product sales) and several columns for expenses, such as automobile, office supplies, permits and licenses, and advertising, among others. I've included an example list for ongoing income and expenses for a one year period here:

**Income (by source)**
Pet sitting$30,000
Dog Walking $5,000

Total $35,000

**Expenses**

Legal and accounting (for business plan creation) $100
Insurance $200
Business License and Permits $200
Advertising $200
Web site maintenance $300
Office Supplies $400
Computer Hardware and Software Maintenance $200
Cell phone contract $500
Loan payments $200
Memberships $100
Payroll if you have employees ????
Automobile expenses $12,000

Total $14,400

**Net Income (Income minus Expenses) $20,600**

The other way to do accounting is to use a software program. Two commonly used programs are Microsoft Office and Quickbooks. You can't turn these programs on and they'll balance your books. You need to create the list of accounts you want to use and use them to input expenses.

To keep any accounting system running, you'll likely need to devote at least an hour weekly or a half day each month. And, don't let it get out of hand by avoiding it. If you let it pile up, you will just have a bigger job at the end.

If you don't think you are cut out to manage the books, get a book-keeper or accountant to organize it for you. The bonus is that they can generate reports when you need them while you spend your time managing the business. They will also keep the accounting software up to date, which is often a worry for small businesses.

Once you have the books in order, the next step is creating reports. There are many and I'm going to define them, but which ones you generate will depend on what information you want and what you are doing with it.

I get a profit and loss statement each month for my business. It tells me how much I've taken in (revenue) and how much I've paid out (expenses). This is a good one because it tells you the profit or loss in a particular period. This could be a month, a year, or any-thing in-between. You can also compare a month to the same month last year. It also tells you how much money you can safely take out in wages.

A balance sheet is a listing of the company's assets and liabilities. In simple terms, what you own and what you owe. If you find that the assets are increasing, you are on solid footing. If your liabilities are growing, then you need to make more money or cut expenses.

The cash flow statement reviews simply how much money came in and how much went out. This one is useful if you are trying to explain what is going on in your checking account.

## Bookkeepers and Accountants

Should you hire help with the number-crunching? I've mentioned both bookkeepers and accountants. A bookkeeper can help you track expenses and income and prepare monthly and quarterly statements. This is certainly work that you can do. I did it for the first few years for my business, but I found that a bookkeeper can do it better and faster than me. In the early years, that may be all you need if you want to do your taxes yourself. The side benefit of bookkeepers is that they back up your data so it is secure.

As the business grows and/or you don't want to do any of the income/expense tracking or the taxes, you can consider an accountant. They can often provide bookkeeping services (or you can use someone separate), but they excel at keeping finances in order.

Accountants make tax time easier. There are many rules to follow and they seem to change every year. Yes, you can keep up to date yourself with government web sites, but be prepared to spend a lot of time wading through the regulations and forms. My recommendation is – get help!

You will also find that having an accountant on board can help you garner more funds from a bank because the bank sees the professionalism you are exuding.

Choosing a bookkeeper or accountant is a personal thing. You can work off recommendations or ask other small business owners who they use and why. And, you can ask anyone you are considering what their experience is with pet sitters or small businesses.

Look at this seriously because it will likely be a long-term relationship.

# Borrowing

I've put together a start-up cost sheet to give you examples of what your initial costs may be. These estimates vary greatly with where you live and what you plan to do, but you can use this form and change the numbers to suit you. This form just has the costs you will incur to set up. It does not include ongoing expenses such as car expense.

**Start-Up Expenses Worksheet**
Initial Market research
-(trips to veterinarians and pet stores, phone calls, data collection) $100
Legal and accounting (for business plan creation) $400
Insurance $200
Business License $100
Advertising $200
Web site design $500

**Equipment:**
First Aid Kit (human and animal) $100
Dog leashes and collars $ 50
Dog muzzles (set) $ 50
Cat litter $ 10

**Office Set Up**
Computer and Printer $1400
Desk and Chair $500
Cell phone contract $300
Stationary and tools $300

Total $4,210

Don't panic if you don't have money in your pocket. The logical place to start to get financing like this is to ask friend and family. The next place is banks that lend money to people starting businesses. In some cases, you may even be able to get a grant. If you don't have assets to back up the loan, you will likely need a cosigner, or perhaps you have a partner that has money that can fund it.

Once you get the business going, you'll need operating money, also called operating capital. This pays expenses while you can't, when your income is still low. In time, the business generates its own capital to operate with, but until then, you need a source to draw on. If you are borrowing, this is usually part of the package a bank gives to you.

## Client Billing

Most pet sitters generate client invoices. This allows you to keep a record of your visits, but also track income. This can be done manually and with a computer, using a program for invoicing. Some pet sitting software can do all this and allow you to accumulate a client history, integrating their file into the system. This can be useful for impressing your clients.

Here's an example. If Mrs. Smith calls and wants you to look after Misty, you can ask – "Is Misty still on that medication for her bladder?" It shows you are paying attention, and she thinks you have an elephant's memory. Also, if you and the owner discussed a change last time, the computer can help remind you that the client was thinking about two walks a day rather than one. You might be able to sell more services.

A personal touch is to add a written note to any invoice you give to the client. You can tell them that Sandy (the cat) was especially good this time and even came out to play.

And, how are clients going to pay you? Normally, you would accept cash and checks. In these days of on-line payments, you can also have your clients pay through PayPal or a credit card through your bank merchant services. You can arrange card payments through a local bank, but there is a major disadvantage—they take between two and four percent of the total in addition to a monthly fee. These fees are continually changing, so if you are considering it, talk to the bank. But, using cards does put the money directly into your account the same day.

When we talk about clients paying you, we unfortunately have to talk about collections. Don't let a client "forget" to pay you and let the amount they owe you mount up. You have your expenses, so you need to get the money to pay them.

If a client hasn't paid you, don't take on another job with them unless it is cleared up. If you are still nervous about them, ask for a deposit on the next job. I know this is hard for some people. You probably hate asking someone for money. My advice is – get over it. You can't give away your expertise and, if they don't pay you, in my mind, they don't value your services.

If you've asked and the client just won't pay, your only option is to send the account to a collection agency. They try to collect the money on your behalf from the debtor. They charge a fee and you may end up paying them half of any money they recover, but I look at it this way—it's out of your hands and you don't have to think about it any more. You can find collection agencies listed in the yellow pages.

One way to avoid payment problems is to have set payment policies. Most pet sitters ask for payment in advance or at the time service is rendered, usually the first day of the contract. Remember, if it all goes right, you won't see the client, so it may be inconvenient to get the money from them after the fact. Tell them about your payment policy when you have your introductory meeting. Any other time is too late.

While going over fees and payment policies, you may want to explain your cancellation policy. If you have booked the client for a holiday weekend and, most importantly, turned away other business because of that commitment, you'll lose if they cancel. Some pet sitters ask for 50 percent to be paid on bookling; some ask for all. You may want to credit part of it to a future job with that client. What you ultimately do will be up to you, but you should get something to make up for the loss you suffer.

Now is a good time to talk about your fees, specifically how often should you review them? Most pet sitters do this annually. If you think about it, your expenses go up every year. I've never yet seen them go down. Automobile expenses rise with higher gas prices. Your employees (if you have them) always want a raise. Your cost of living has also risen.

So, set a date on your calendar to review fees. This could be annually. You can also do it every six months. When you look at fees, you have to be objective. Don't start thinking that your clients won't like it if you raise your day rate by $1.50. If you raise fees, it's possible that a thrifty client will leave you, but if you are providing the service, they will stay. Pet sitting is a good deal for the client! Where else can they get someone as committed and trustworthy as you looking after their loved one and their home?

# Business Plan

A business plan is a formal statement of a company's financial and operations goals and benchmarks.

You may wonder if you really need a business plan. You do. The reason is that you want to know what to expect. It is a map for your business over the next few years. If you show a business plan to a prospective lender, and it shows that you can make a viable business, there is a greater chance you are going to get the money.

But, the major function of a business plan is to gauge if you are on track. By using your business plan as you grow, you can see where you went right and where you may have gone wrong. If you find yourself slow at any time, you can refer to the plan and find out what you need to do to get back on track.

So, how can we start? What goes into a business plan?

The first section is the summary. The section spells out what business you are going to create. It is an overview, so details aren't necessary at this stage. It could be as simple as "The ABC Pet Sitting Service is going to provide dog and cat pet sitting in Cavendish County."

Next, a lender will want to see an industry overview. There are two points for this. One is for the reader to learn about the industry and see if they want to invest in your business (loan you money). But, the other point is that they want to see if YOU understand the business. If you can list statistics that show how pet sitting is growing; it makes it more viable.

In this section, include how the industry is changing. For example, find figures on how consumers are spending more and more on pet services each year. Find out how many other pet sitters are in the area. If they are all successful businesses, it shows there is room for one more. You may also want to get a handle on how many pets there are in the area. You can also ask veterinarians and pet stores how they are doing to get an idea if you have an expanding or shrinking market.

The next thing to include is your credentials. Lenders want to see what your experience is with animals, but also what skills you can bring for managing a small business. List the jobs you have had and what skills you have acquired. For example, if you worked in a marketing firm, how can you use that expertise in marketing a pet sitting business? If you were a customer service representative, what people skills did you learn that can help you succeed? The lender wants to see what skills you have to make the business succeed.

An operating overview shows how you will set up your business. For example, how will you perform your duties? Do you have an office? Is it at home or rented space? What financial help do you need? What support do you have if you need assistance in providing your service?

Definitely include a section on how you are going to market your services. And, how do you attract and retain clients? List your important qualities that make you suited to own and run a pet sitting business. If you have a partner, include his or her qualifications as well.

The hardest part to do in your business plan, unless you thrive on numbers, is the financials. This is a forecast of the revenue and expenses for the first three, and possibly the first five years of operation. You will want projections of these two categories and a balance sheet that shows the difference between the two.

There are many sources for help in generating a business plan. You can find books on home-based businesses. There are websites with lots of good ideas. Pet sitting organizations may provide a template for you to follow, and you can just tailor it to your needs. There are also college and internet courses on the topic.

When writing your own plan, don't get too carried away. Business plans should be only a few pages unless you are planning on creating a pet sitting empire.

Definitely include start-up expenses and ongoing expenses. Having these financials in the business plan is very important. Even if you have a rich uncle (or another family member) that can supply funds to get you going, they probably want to see if you have done your homework and can prove you can make it profitable.

If you need money and have to approach a financial institution, even though it is a daunting task, think of it in the right light. They want you to succeed so that they can get their money back but they also want you to make it as well. If you can show them financials that exude success, they will lend you money. Be prepared with all the data they require.

There are some other things you can include in your business plan, but perhaps we should call them "goals". For example, you may want to state that you will generate proper forms for customer contracts (perhaps with the help of a lawyer) within the first six months. Maybe you want to become insured and set that goal at a year. Perhaps you have marketing goals to expand the business after it's been running for a while to justify an employee. You might want to create back-up plans. For example, if you are away, what can you do so that the business can run smoothly in your absence?

A business plan is what you put into it. It can be incredibly detailed, or just contain the bare essentials. I'm sure you have your own idea of what you want in it. You may want to prove that the business will be self-sufficient. The more detail you include, the better you'll know if you are on target.

Even if you aren't going to the bank for money, it's a good idea to create a business plan. Remember, this is going to be your roadmap on how to run your business. I recommend doing it for the first year, but you can certainly go farther.

Here are the components and how to write them in.

• Summary—a quick run-down on the business you are creating. This can be just a line or two.

• Industry Overview—an education for the reader describing what the business is so they can see why it is viable. You may want to include the number of veterinary hospitals, kennels, and pet sitters in your area. This reveals what the potential market can be.

• Credentials—this is where you have to shine as the best person to start a pet sitting business. List your education and your experience that makes it a slam-dunk that you can do this.

• Operating Overview—this tells the reader how you plan to approach and run the business. Include how you are going to do your marketing.

• Financials—these tell the reader what your income and expenses are going to be so they can see what money you are going to take home. You can forecast income by taking a logical guess at how many visits you might be doing each month for the first year. For expenses, break them into start-up expenses and ongoing expenses.

• Miscellaneous—list the other things you might do (get a partner, hire an employee, add another service)

# Canine Feeding

It's probably pretty obvious that when you're caring for a dog, you'll be feeding it. But so many questions remain: How much? What kind of food? How often? And what about water? Let's exploreg these questions and develop some guidelines to ensure that your four-footed wards are happy and healthy before, during, and after that favorite time of the day, mealtime.

So to begin, let's set one basic rule: Give the dog exactly what the owner tells you. Don't vary it. If you take it on yourself to improve the diet, you could end up with a dog suffering from indigestion or a life-threatening disease such as pancreatitis. By the time you're looking after your canine clients, you should already have a good sense of how their owners want them fed. (It's something you'll cover in your initial client meeting).

Like people, dogs have preferences for what, when, and how they like to eat. And they can get conditioned to expect certain circumstances.

Let me demonstrate this point with a story. When I was in veterinary college, I was in charge of a wonderful Standard Poodle called Tiberius (named for Star Trek's James Tiberius Kirk). He was recovering from surgery for bloat. My job was to examine him daily and give him medication, but also to feed him. I dutifully put the special, easy-to-digest canned food in front of him, and though he looked like he wanted it, he wouldn't eat. The next day, I tried again. Same result.

I called the owner and told her that Tiberius seemed to be doing fine, but he wouldn't eat. I'll always remember what she said —"You did tape his ears up didn't you?" The owner taped the ears up so that the flaps wouldn't drag in the food and get dirty. As soon as I did that, he ate ravenously.

Some dogs get fed in certain, sometimes unique, ways. Find out if the owner soaks the dry food, if the dry food is mixed with canned or in separate bowls, or if the canned food is fed first. Is there a special spot where the dog likes to eat? You get the idea—ask the owner.

Also, find out if the dog inhales his food or if he is a grazer. This way, you won't be alarmed and calling the veterinarian if he doesn't eat right away. If there is more than one dog, do they eat different foods and are they fed away from or next to each other?

So it sounds like the owner is your first and best source for how much to feed a dog. But sometimes you might misunderstand their directions, or perhaps the owner miscommunicated their desires to you.

Here's an example: A pet sitter I know was given written instructions by a dog owner that said to feed the pet 2 cups of food daily. The pet sitter split this into two portions for two meals, thus giving the 90-pound (about 40 kilograms) Labrador his one cup twice daily.

If you know big dogs, you can probably see the problem already. The poor dog was starving. Thankfully, she called me and asked if the amount was appropriate. I told her to double it right away. The owners had meant to write 2 cups twice daily, not 2 cups daily. If you doubt the instructions, always confirm them with the owner, or ask a professional for advice.

And just to make sure you have a good sense of when your instructions are right on the money, or when they might be off, here are some (very rough) guidelines for approximate amounts to feed dogs. The amounts are based on feeding exclusively dry or canned. But, you can use the same numbers and mix them up. For example, a 65-pound dog could have 1-1/2 cups of dry food and 2-1/4 tins of canned food daily.

DESIGN TABLE

| Dog weight | Dry Food | Canned Food* |
|---|---|---|
|  |  |  |
| 10 pounds (5 kilograms) | 3/4 cup | 1 can |
| 30 pounds (15 kilograms) | 1-2/3 cups | 2-2/3 cans |
| 65 pounds (30 kilograms) | 3 cups | 4-1/2 cans |
| 100 pounds (45 kilograms) | 4-1/3 cups | 6 cans |

* assume 13 ounce/370 gram can

Notice that the amount is not directly related to weight. As dogs get bigger, the amount they need per pound falls. This is because the metabolic rate is faster in small dogs than large dogs. Think of the difference between a hummingbird and an elephant—the hummingbird must eat almost its own body weight in food daily to meet its needs. The elephant eats just a small portion of its weight.

The amount needed also differs with the quality of the food (higher quality/less needed) and activity of the dog (more active/more food needed). But, the best measure of whether or not you are satisfying needs is to weigh the dog and see if weight is stable. If weight drops, you need to feed more. A dog that gains needs less food. As a pet sitter, you'll only do this if you have a long-term contract for pet sitting a dog.

The amount of food needed is also impacted by diseases that the dog might have. If you have a diabetic dog, he likely needs more a healthy dog. On the other hand, a hypothyroid dog has a slow metabolic rate and can survive on less food.

Then there is appetite. Most dogs, given the chance, will eat themselves into oblivion. Here's a rough way to help you decide if you are feeding to much—look at the poop, scientifically known as stool or feces. If the poop is hard and dry, you are not feeding enough. If its soft and the dog is healthy otherwise, you may be feeding too much.

## Water

As you know, food is only half of the diet equation. Water is also an essential part of nutrition. Here's something to consider. We humans drink for two reasons. One is because we are thirsty. The other is because we are told to (eight glasses every day) or because we want another jolt of coffee. Dogs, on the other hand, unless you are offering tasty beef stock, drink only because they have to satisfy their thirst—they only drink because they have to.

So you need to give dogs as much as they want. Never withhold water from a dog. You may be tempted to do this if the dog has a habit of peeing in the house. If you do this, you can quickly run into trouble. The owner may tell you how much the dog requires each day. Whatever it is, leave twice that amount down in case the bowl gets spilt or the calculation was off.

The most common sign of a medical problem is drinking too much. Drinking too little water is rarely a concern unless you have a sick dog that is getting dehydrated. If you notice that a dog is drinking excessively, mention it to the owner. Excessive thirst can be the first sign of diabetes. These dogs also tend to overeat or be hungry as well. Other conditions that can cause dogs to drink more are kidney failure and Cushing's Disease.

The cut off we use for medical purposes is if they drink more than 50 milliliters (about one ounce) for each pound of body weight daily, we have a problem. Small dogs weighing 20 pounds should drink less than 1000 milliliters (about 4 cups). I've seen some larger dogs (80 pounds) with kidney problems consume a gallon and a half in a day.

## The Obese Dog

Suppose you are pet sitting an obese dog. You know that weight reduction is in the pet's best interest, but should you go ahead and diet him? I have some clients that are very resistant to taking advice on how to manage weight issues in their pets. In fact, some use their overweight pet as something to brag about, such as "my dog is over 100 pounds."

I know the frustration I feel in these circumstances, and you will probably feel the same way. A fat dog can hardly move without wheezing; the huge cat can't jump up or play and will likely become diabetic.

But, it comes down to the wishes of the owner. You can certainly ask the client if they want you to help get their pet's weight down while they are on holiday. But, unless they agree, don't take it into your own hands.

## Prescription Foods

Prescription foods are available to prevent bladder stones, help a dog cope with kidney disease, boost brain performance, ease the pain in arthritic joints, and reduce salt so the heart is not taxed, just to name a few. As you go about your pet sitting career, you will see pets on these special diets. Don't memorize what each one is for, but you should know why your client is feeding a certain diet. It makes you sound knowledgeable.

If you have a client feeding one of these special diets, don't change it and don't add treats, just in case there are allergies to the treats.

## Treats

Most owners supply treats for you to give. Only give these treats and in the quantity the owner tells you. You don't want to give unfamiliar treats in case the dog reacts to them (diarrhea and food allergies). You also don't want to overfeed and get the dog fat.

Some owners are fastidious about food and treats. I've seen some clients count the treats so they can see if the pert sitter followed their directions. If you are supposed to have three left when they get home, they'd better be there.

# Feline Nutrition

How often you feed depends on two things - the type of food you're feeding and the cat herself. If you are feeding dry food, it can be left out all day and won't go "bad". Canned food, on the other hand, will. It will dry out (and cats won't eat it), or bacteria will grow in it and cause food poisoning. For this reason, wet food (both canned and other types) needs to be fed twice daily.

What do you do with the other half can of wet food? If you put it in the fridge, some cats refuse to eat it. You can get around this two ways. One is to warm the food in the microwave to what I call mouse temperature. You don't want it too hot because cats don't like that either. The other option is to keep it at room temperature. I do this at home. I feed four cats and I put a lid on the leftover half can and feed it later in the day. If it's hot weather, I don't do it, but in the colder seasons, it works just fine. I don't use food over 12 hours old; I throw it away.

Some owners feed a mixture of dry and canned foods. Hopefully, the cat eats the wet food first and then, over the day, the dry food. This leads us into delving into how cats eat.

There are two types of cats - the finicky eaters and the ones that eat all they can, as fast as they can.

When feeding dry food, you'll find that some are addicted to it. I'm not sure if it's the texture or the taste, but they crave it. It's like me and popcorn - I can't eat just one piece. With cats, they dive into the food and eat their fill. The problem is that if they eat too much, it leads to obesity.

They can also overload the stomach and end up vomiting the whole meal right back up. Simply changing to canned food can sometimes stop these cats from vomiting. Canned food is 80 percent water. While dry food physically expands as it absorbs digestive juices that enter the stomach, canned food stays about the same size and doesn't put pressure on the stomach wall.

If I have a client and their cat is vomiting after inhaling dry food, I suggest limiting food intake (more meals per day) or feeding canned food.

Dog food should not be fed to cats. For starters, it is too low in protein and fat (and also high in carbohydrates - I'll get into this shortly), but more importantly, it lacks sufficient taurine. This amino acid is essential for cats and cat food is supplemented with it. Cats eating dog food deficient in taurine can suffer from heart disease and blindness. Of course, if a cat eats mainly cat food, a few pieces of dog food now and then won't hurt.

## The Best Foods for Cats

Views on feline nutrition have changed radically in recent years. Veterinarians have realized that cats thrive on a high protein/high fat/low carbohydrate diet. If you remember a diet touted for people a few years back called the Atkins Diet, this would sound familiar. I jokingly call it the Catkins Diet.

The dry diet we've been feeding for decades is cereal-based which is, of course, high in carbohydrates. You may wonder why this is included in cat food? If you think of cats in ancient times, they were used to guard the granary, not eat the contents. They showed no interest in the grain. The reason manufacturers use grain is because of cost. They can buy grain much cheaper than they can buy meat.

We now know that diet containing this level of carbohydrate can lead to obesity and a predisposition to diabetes. Cats do far better on low carb diets. They tend to shed weight, put on more muscle, and thrive.

You can use this knowledge when you talk to your clients. Tell them what the best diet is and then tell them how to feed such a diet. You can do this by reading labels. Look for foods that have meat as the first two or three ingredients. If they have corn, wheat, or rice in there, be wary.

Canned food has another big plus. It contains between 75 and 80 percent moisture, so it boosts water intake. You may wonder why this is important.

Cats are desert animals. They can concentrate their urine so that they don't lose excess water when it is scarce. This was driven home when I read a case report of a cat that crawled into a dresser when her owners were moving. They didn't see her and assumed she had ran away. The dresser came out of storage over a month later. The cat survived. In contrast, a person can't do this; we'd be dead after just a few days without water.

Though cats can limit water loss, it can lead to problems. The main issue is that they form crystals in the concentrated urine. These crystals can move out the bladder into the urethra of male cats and block them. This creates an emergency.

The water contained in canned food dilutes the urine, reducing the tendency for crystals to form. It means a healthier bladder.

What quantity should you feed cats? The average cat, which is about 10 pounds, should eat about a cup of dry food. If you are feeding canned, the same cat would get one tin (5.5 ounces or 156 grams) per day. Bigger cats need more and smaller cats need less. Activity level also affects requirements. Active cats need more and sedentary cats, who are usually older cats, don't need as much.

Another diet I want to bring up, and it is used in both dogs and cats, is the raw diet. This is a meat (with or without bone) diet fed with the goal to better approximate the natural diet of these animals. Raw diets are hotly debated as to their benefits and dangers (carrying bacteria that can infect people).

You may find that some of your clients are feeding raw food. If your client feeds this way, ask them how they want the food handled. Each one will have a different way of storing, preparing, and feeding. Think of it this way—if you were handling raw meat that you are going to eat, what would you do to keep it from spoiling? Simply use the same principles.

## Cats and Water

Like dogs, cats need water. But, the amount varies with the food you are feeding and if they have any diseases.

My cats, which are fed canned food exclusively, hardly seem to drink. In fact, if I see one of them drinking, I wonder if there is a problem. They get most of the water they need from the food. On the other hand, cats that are on dry food need to drink. In hot weather they drink more. In cold, wet weather, they drink less.

Cats fed dry food will drink more water from ther bowl. But, they only drink what they have to and they are chronically dehydrated. This can be a contributor to crystals in the urine.

Cats with kidney disease (which strikes about 1/3 of older cats), drink more because they can't concentrate their urine. The same holds true with cats suffering from uncontrolled diabetes. The difference is that while both diseases tend to cause weight loss, kidney cats eat less while diabetic cats tend to eat more.

The best way to monitor urine production and also see how much a cat is drinking, is to watch the litter box. You will get to know how much an average cat pees in one go. In clumping litter, it usually forms a 1.5 inch (4 centimeter) ball. If it's bigger, suspect a problem. Cats with kidney disease or diabetes form huge "pee balls" in their clumping litter or they flood the granular litter. Tell the owner so they can get the cat checked. They may think large amounts of urine are normal.

A cat with kidney disease must drink lots of water to prevent dehydration. Even just a little dehydration reduces their drive to drink, which can start a vicious cycle. The stress of the owners leaving can put this cycle into motion, as well as any health ailment.

If you feel a cat is not drinking enough, here are some ideas to encourage water intake. We've already looked at feeding canned food. You can also change from tap water to bottled water. Some cats prefer bottled water, shying away from water containing chlorine.

Another thing to do is add more water bowls. This helps in multi-cat households where a dominant cat may control access to the single water bowl. One of my cats likes a glass of water on the bathroom counter. I refresh it every morning and night. Some cats like to drink from a dripping tap. Other cats like ice added to the water to cool it down. I haven't yet met a cat that likes warm or hot water. There are even cat fountains available that filter and cool the water.

If you thought watering a cat was just filling a bowl, you now know better!

# Assessing Health of Cats and Dogs - the Vital Signs

How can we tell if a dog or cat we're looking after is healthy? We look at the vital signs - the signposts to health. These are the first things veterinarians check when you go in with a sick pet. They tell the doctor how the body is working, and if something is awry, what diseases or conditions to suspect. You can use the same vital signs to assess the pets you look after. It will help you decide if a veterinary visit is needed.

The vital signs that you can check are:

- Temperature

- Pulse rate

- Respiratory rate

- Mucus membrane color

- Skin turgor

Temperature

Buy a digital thermometer from the drug store and label it "for pet use only". You are going to put it in the anus, so you don't want to get it mixed up with yours. You can apply a little Vaseline, oil, or liquid soap to the metal tip for lubrication. Insert it as far as you can comfortably. Don't worry - the thermometer widens so you can't push it in too far. If it's not far enough in, it won't register the true body temperature. I hold the tail up with one hand and hold the thermometer in the other.

Most digital thermometers "beep" once they have recorded the temperature. At this point, remove it and read the display. Normal body temperature for dogs is between 38.0 and 39.2 Celsius (100.5 and 102.5 Fahrenheit). Clean the thermometer tip by wiping with a tissue. Sterilize it with a second tissue soaked with rubbing alcohol.

If the pet's temperature is high, he has a fever or is suffering from hyperthermia—exposure to too much heat. A low temperature means hypothermia. This can happen if a patient is chilled, but also with dehydration or severe illness. This suggests he's got a problem and needs attention.

Normal body temperature for cats is between 38.2 and 39.2 Celsius (100.5 and 102.5 Fahrenheit). Dogs easily get overheated on a hot day. Cats, not so much. Cats sleep when it's hot while dogs will still run after a ball. Most people consider this a reflection of their intelligence!

Pulse Rate

The pulse rate or heart rate is the number of beats per minute. Of course, you can hear it with a stethoscope, but you can also feel it by putting your hand on the chest between the forelegs or feeling the pulse in the large (femoral) artery that runs on the inside of the back leg.

Count the beats in 15 seconds, multiply by four, and you have the rate per minute. Most dogs have a pulse rate between 80 and 140. It rises if excited and slows down when sleeping. A high pulse rate suggests a fever or heart disease. A low rate can also be seen with heart disease, or lack of blood circulation to the heart.

Cat heart rates tend to be higher than dogs and they are quick to react to stress. Resting heart rates are 100 to 140 beats per minute. But, if you hold a cat against his will or stress him, you can easily drive the heart rate above 200. It is very difficult to feel and count a pulse going that fast. You will need a stethoscope.

Older cats (over 10 years of age) are susceptible to a disease called hyperthyroidism, where a benign tumor grows in the thyroid gland. Physically, it doesn't cause a problem, but it produces thyroid hormone that speeds up metabolism. The consequence is that heart rate also goes up, well over 200.

Respiratory Rate

Respiratory rate (RR) is the number of breaths per minute. This is easy to measure. Just watch the ribs or the abdomen rising and falling. Count how many times it does the up/down cycle in 15 seconds and again multiply by four.

Panting is normal if a dog is excited or too warm (it's how they lose body heat). You'll see the chest quickly moving in and out with shallow breaths. On the other hand, if you see a dog breathing hard with its abdomen pumping with each breath, something is amiss.

Different cats breathe at very different rates. Some breathe 10 times a minute, but a cat I have (Curbee – she was found by the curb) breathes at a resting rate of about 25. It's normal for her.

In both species, the thing to watch is the abdomen. If you see the abdomen working to pull air into the chest, there could be a lung problem. Unfortunately, the most common reason is a tumor or infection in the chest which causes fluid accumulation. There is simply no room left for the lungs to expand. The other condition that makes breathing hard is asthma. I've never seen a dog with this disease, but I've diagnosed many cats with it.

If you see a cat panting with its mouth open, it is most likely due to stress. Only rarely does it suggest overheating. I sometimes see cats panting after a car ride to my office. At home, you rarely see cats panting. If you do, maybe the cat just got chased by a dog or had a close encounter with a car. If it continues, it's a problem and needs checking.

Mucus Membrane Color

Pull the dog's lip up and peer at the gums. Mucus membrane color is an indicator of health. It should be pink. Have a look in the mirror and look at the color of your gums - that's the color you want to see.

Excessively red gums can indicate a high body temperature (fever or overheating), or gum disease. Pale gums indicate anemia or poor blood flow from low blood pressure. Yellow gums suggest liver problems or hemolytic anemia where the red blood cells are being destroyed. The membranes should also be moist. If they feel tacky, it indicates dehydration.

Skin Turgor

This is a test to determine the water content in the body. Grasp the skin over the shoulders and pull it up. Once you've "tented" the skin, let it go and see how fast it returns to a normal position. You can also twist the skin to see a little more clearly what is going on.

If a pet is dehydrated, the skin takes longer to fall back down. Don't go too high on the neck (towards the head) because a skin test there can make it look like a dog or cat is dehydrated when it isn't. Once you've done a few, you can see what is normal. If the skin is slow to return to normal and the gums are also tacky, it confirms dehydration.

You can detect dehydration in cats just as you do in dogs by doing a skin tent test. I find this the most valuable of the vital signs for determining if a cat is ill. If they aren't feeling well, they often reduce their water intake and get dehydrated.

In older cats, the skin seems to lose some of its elasticity so you may think it is dehydrated when it is not. If you are unsure, look at the entire picture. Are the gums tacky and is the cat drinking? These give you additional clues to make a decision to whether or not the cat needs veterinary care.

## How to Use Vital Signs

When would you want to check the vital signs? It's when you are unsure if you have an emergency. Let's suppose you go to check your canine friend and rather than his boisterous self, he's slow to move and he's slow to eat. It might be a temporary problem but you're worried that when you get back late in the day, he could be worse. And, that's when you'd have to take him to the emergency hospital rather than his regular veterinarian. By checking the vitals, you can see if he needs help now.

Things that would trigger your examination are no energy, vomiting and diarrhea, urinating a lot, not wanting to move, which add up to the thing we call "ADR" - ain't doing right. Let's look at cats in a little more detail.

What would make you suspect that there is a health concern in the cat you are looking after? It might be the food is left uneaten. The litter box may be unused or, in the other extreme, there is too much urine or the cat had diarrhea. The cat might be limping or unwilling to get up. In essence, you are looking for any behavior that is not normal for the cat.

So the next step is to do a cursory examination. Before you touch the cat, watch the breathing. Does it look normal? Then, lift the cat up. If he cries, he may have a fever (check the temperature) or be sore somewhere.

Put the cat on a table or counter. Lift the skin up and see if he is dehydrated. Next, check the gums for color. Pulse rate is mainly used by veterinarian, but if you can take it, it can provide good information.

When is it an emergency? I feel that if a cat won't eat, has a fever, is vomiting or has diarrhea, is breathing hard, or is limping, you need a professional assessment.

# Vaccinations

Thoughts on vaccines differ between veterinarians so there is no one consistent view on what animals require for vaccines. Some people don't vaccinate their pets. Others get the vaccines done and keep them up to date.

There are no legal requirements for vaccines unless you live in a place where rabies vaccines are mandated. Some pet sitters require proof of rabies vaccines, but the need for this really depends on where you live. In some areas, is not a risk. In others, it is a concern.

The issue is that rabies is the only canine disease that you can die from. The best way to gauge the risk to you is to ask your veterinarian if the disease is in your area. You can also ask them what they advise for vaccinations.

But, asking clients to have their dogs vaccinated could put you in a position where they decide not to use you if they don't want to bother getting the vaccines done. It will then be up to you to refuse taking a client if they don't want to follow your "rules".

If the pet is going to kennels or doggie day care, the facility may insist on some vaccines. These normally include distemper, parvovirus, hepatitis, parainfluenza, and Bordetella. The last two are causes of the kennel cough or canine cough complex.

What you will find is that most people take vaccinations seriously, which may mean they get them done or have their good reasons for not having them done. In both instances, they care about their dogs and they make excellent pet sitting clients. Some people use pet sitters because they don't want to meet the kennel requirements on vaccines.

What about cats and their vaccinations? Like dogs, there are no mandated vaccinations for cats unless you live in one of the few places where rabies is required by law. The rest are optional from a legal perspective.

You will find that more cat owners than dog owners do not get regular vaccines done. There are several reasons for this. One is that many cats are frequently indoors and don't go outside. The chances they are going to be threatened with a disease is quite low. In fact, the only diseases that can be transmitted to an indoor cat are panleukopenia and the respiratory viruses calicivirus and rhinotracheitis. You could carry panleukopenia on your shoes as it is passed in the feces of infected cats. With the respiratory viruses, it would mean you would have to get licked or sneezed on by a cat that is shedding the virus and then have the second cat lick it off your fingers. Rabies risk is based on exposure to the natural host for rabies in your area.

But, the other reason some cat owners avoid vaccines is because of the threat of a cancerous tumor called a fibrosarcoma. These tumors are linked to injections (any injections, not just vaccines). The incidence is between 2 and 8 per 10,000 injections.

# Canine Health Problems

This is where you can shine as a pet sitter. You may be able to spot a problem before the client does. You might see the dog bother her right ear. Maybe he's lame on his left hind leg. This can lead to an earlier diagnosis and faster resolution of the problem.

The other time you can help is when there is a critical illness. Recognizing an emergency may mean the difference between life and death.

The key is to be observant. You don't have a lot of time with each dog, so pay attention! Watch how the dog moves, what it does, how it eats or drinks, and if there are any odors that seem strange.

I'm not going to get into treatment of the diseases we find. That's the veterinarian's job. But, we are going to cover what to look for that tells you when a veterinary visit is needed.

Eyes

Let's start with the head, specifically, the eyes. This is probably the easiest organ system (yes, the eyes are organ) to give advice on. If you spot an eye problem, it is an emergency and the dog needs to see the veterinarian. Period. Now, that's easy advice to follow, isn't it?

Now I'll tell you the reason. An eye may look irritated, but there are many causes for this. It could be a mild allergy, which itself is not a big problem. But, what if the redness in the eye is due to glaucoma? In this case, the eye pressure has risen to dangerous levels and without fast treatment the dog may end up blind, and certainly has a very painful eye. An ulcer on the surface of the eye, another reason for irritation, can cause rupture of the eye and resulting blindness.

So, if you see any eye problem, it needs checking. Don't try eye drops because some medications are contra-indicated with specific diseases (such as steroids with a corneal ulcer). Always get a diagnosis before treating eye conditions. And, don't try home remedies such as putting a wet, cold teabag on the eye. It may be considered soothing, but if you have a serious disease, the failure to treat it appropriately could end in loss of vision or loss of the eye.

Ears

There are three ways to tell if there is an ear disease. One is seeing the dog scratching his ear or shaking his head. Another is looking at the ear and seeing redness and discharge. The last is smelling the ear. In fact, I use this way to tell me if there is an ear problem all the time.

Put your nose at the entrance to the ear canal (I'm assuming you have a nice dog) and sniff. Normal ears have hardly any odor. If there is a bacterial infection, it smells foul. A sweet odor can suggest a yeast infection.

Teeth

The last thing to check out on the head is the teeth. It's amazing how many people don't seem to recognize oral disease. I'm talking about tartar, infection, and abscessed teeth. You can see dental problems by lifting the lip. But, if you want to know oral health, use your nose again.

You can do this one of two ways. One is putting your nose close to the teeth and smelling. Infected mouths smell like they are, you know, infected. Just smell a few and you'll get the idea. Worried about putting your nose so close? Try this way. Put a small gauze over your finger and rub it on the teeth. Then, smell the gauze. Advising the owner to have the teeth attended to can really boost the health of the dog.

Skin and Skin Parasites

Let's move on to the skin. There are two main things that people notice about skin. One is an itch. The other is hair loss.

If the skin is itchy, the animal scratches and bites. There are lots of reasons for this. If you live in warmer climates, the first thing you'd think of is fleas. These little insects stay on the dog, but lay eggs that fall off into the environment. Once they hatch and go through a larval and pupal stage, they seek out another host. Look for fleas at the base of the hair, mainly above the tail and in the groin. You can also find flea feces (it looks like black pepper) on the skin above the tail.

But, if you live up north and it's January, the last thing you'd suspect is fleas. It's far more likely that the dog has an allergy. These dogs bite their feet, scratch their ears, and generally itch everywhere.

One parasite that you may come across that you need to know about is lice. These little bugs spend their entire life on the host, infesting another host when one dog rubs against another. They can create an intense itch. You can see the lice themselves or their eggs attached to hairs.

Lice are quite rare, but the reason I bring them up is because you can carry them from one dog to another through combs and grooming instruments. If you have a client with a lice-infested dog, take extra care that you don't move the infestation to another of your dog clients. It is even rarer to see lice in cats.

Sore Legs

Can you tell if a dog is lame? There are little clues you can look for to determine if a dog has a sore leg and which leg it is. I must tell you about a pet peeve of mine. I've had clients bring in dogs that are obviously lame with the dog hardly putting weight on the leg. The owner says their dog is not in pain because he never cries. The dog is in pain! He's telling you the best way he can, and he needs help.

If a dog is holding a leg up, it's not too hard to tell which leg is sore. It's the more subtle ones that you need to watch closely. Many people get front leg lamenesses wrong. They can't tell which leg is sore.

Get in front of the dog and watch the head as the dog moves, preferably at a trot. In a male dog, you'll see what we call a head bob. The head goes up when weight is placed on the sore leg and down when the weight is transferred to the sound leg. Try this yourself. If you have a sore left foot, your head will go up when you use that leg and fall down on your good leg.

For a hind leg, the sore leg has a shorter stride (and less time on the ground) than the good leg. The muscles on the sore leg may be shrunken compared to the healthy one. Just put your hand around the muscles from the back of the leg.

You can also see a hip hike where the hip goes up when the weight is on the sore leg. If both back legs are sore, you won't be able to tell. Pets can only limp if they have a good leg that can take the weight.

## Anal Sacs

I'm sure you've seen dogs drop their back end and pull their bum along the ground. Many people still think this is due to worms. If they happen to have a tapeworm infestation, they can cause anal irritation, but it's far more likely to be due to full anal sacs. These are bag-like structures, one on each side of the anus. The solution - have them emptied. Veterinarians will do this for you; so will some groomers.

## Diarrhea

Now let's look at elimination issues. If you see a dog straining to go to the bathroom and no stool is coming out, what is the problem?

If you are like most dog owners, you'll think the dog is constipated, but chances are, you'd be wrong. I've seen constipation in dogs only a few times in my career. It only happens when the dog has eaten bones or wood, and sharp pieces are traveling through the rectum, causing pain. The dog wants to have a bowel movement (BM), but it's too sore.

More commonly, dogs strain hard with no BM coming out because they have diarrhea. Dogs that have diarrhea may pass just a little fluid instead of formed feces. This causes intense irritation. Sometimes you will see blood in the diarrhea. This is not the end of the world. In fact, it is quite common to see blood from the irritation in the colon.

What should you do when you have a dog with diarrhea? If the dog is feeling fine, still wanting to play as well as eat and drink, the first thing you should do is take the food away for one meal and give the intestines a break. If this does not resolve it or the dog is not feeling well, it's best to call the veterinarian.

If you have a dog with diarrhea, is it safe to give a medication like Pepto-Bismol? It is probably safe, but I'd advise against it. When you do this, you are taking on the role of the veterinarian and you are diagnosing and treating the disease. By giving a home remedy like Pepto-Bismol, you alone have determined that the diarrhea is not severe enough to warrant a veterinary visit. You may be right and the dog will recover, but there is a small chance that things could go wrong. Whenever an animal is ill, you can't go wrong by taking them to the veterinarian and certainly can't be at fault, no matter what happens.

## True Canine Emergencies

Knowing some of the common emergencies can mean the difference between life and death.

Bloat

One of the worst diseases I know is gastric dilatation-volvulus, commonly known as bloat. This is a disease of large, deep-chested dogs. Any dog matching this criteria can get it, but it is rampant in Great Danes, Saint Bernards, and German Shepherds.

For some reason, the stomach enlarges from the accumulation of air, and it twists. The entrance and exit are cut off, causing the stomach to get even bigger. This stops blood flow back to the heart and inhibits breathing.

The problem with bloat is that it can kill a dog within hours. The circulation fails and the dog goes into shock. If you see a dog trying to vomit, its abdomen enlarging, or its back end getting weak, consider this disease. Get help as soon as you can.

## Seizures

If you see your first seizure in a dog, it can be unnerving, but you need to keep calm. A seizure is when there is uncontrolled muscle movement. Some dogs flop on their sides with all four legs stiff. Sometimes, they defecate, urinate, and even vomit.

What should you do? Start by making sure the dog does not hurt himself. Pull him into the center of the room away from furniture and stairs. Keep your hands (and other body parts) away from the teeth. You can move the dog safely by pulling a hind leg so you don't get bitten.

The seizure lasts about 15 seconds in most cases. After, they can seem disoriented and can't walk well. This can last five minutes to an hour. As long as the dog only has one seizure, you are in the clear. If they repeat and several occur in a row, the dog needs medication to stop them. I usually give an intravenous injection of Valium to halt the seizures.

## Reverse Sneeze

I get calls every week about reverse sneezing. The client tells me that the dog is snorting/coughing/gagging/sneezing. They have a really difficult time explaining it.

In this case, the dog is inhaling quickly through the nose and then exhaling through the mouth. It is dramatic and the owner often thinks that if it continues, the dog will die. But, the sneezing only lasts for five to ten seconds at the most. Then, the dog is perfectly normal.

The trick is to be able to recognize this unique thing that dogs do. There is no cause for it and no treatment. Do an internet search for "canine reverse sneeze" and you can find videos that show you what it is.

# Feline Health Problems

Eye Disorders

Eye disorders in cats are unlike those in dogs. When we see eye infections (usually due to viruses like Herpesvirus), they are dramatic and the membranes of the eye are swollen. As with dogs, if you see any eye condition, get it checked.

Ear Disorders

Cats rarely get ear problems like dogs. They usually come down to two causes. One is ear mites. These are seen mainly in kittens. Older cats normally develop immunity and get rid of them. We can treat ear mites easily with one or two treatments of special drops.

In older cats, ear problems can be due to growths in the ear canal. You will need a veterinarian to diagnose these.

Fleas and Skin Ailments

Cats are the natural host for fleas. You are probably wondering why I said this. While dogs can react badly to fleas, cats can be covered in fleas, their eggs, and flea feces, and you may not see them scratch at all. Some people say their cats have no fleas, but it is based on seeing no irritation from these parasites.

To check for fleas, part the hair above the tail and look for fleas and flea feces.

Blocked cats

By blocked, I'm referring to the urinary system and I'm talking about male cats. This is not a female feline disease.

Cats, as I mentioned, have a propensity to form crystals in the urine if they don't drink enough water. These crystals can get stuck in the narrow urethra as is runs through the male's penis. Females, with their wider urethra, just pass the crystals out with the urine.

A urethral blockage stops urine flow. The bladder fills and, as pressure mounts, it halts urine production by the kidneys. Once this occurs, the kidneys can't rid the body of toxins and it poisons the cat. He stops eating and drinking and is extremely lethargic. Given time, the cat eventually starts convulsing, goes into a coma, and dies.

Continually be on the lookout for this disease in the male cats you look after. Look for a cat that tries to go to the bathroom, but can't. They often cry as they try to urinate. It is a characteristic, deep moan that you will recognize once you've heard it. You may see him straining in the litterbox, but a common place they try and pee is the bathtub. I think it's because the tub is cold and they rest their inflamed penis on it, but that's just my guess.

Every time you clean the litter box, look for evidence that the cat urinated. If there is no wet spot or clump there, be suspicious. If the cat is blocked, he may also be off his food and acting uncomfortable. Some are sensitive if you pick them up by the belly (pressure on a full bladder).

A blocked cat is a true emergency—he can die within 72 hours of the first sign. If you suspect this disease, get the cat checked. The veterinarian will unblock the cat and then start him on a preventive program to stop the disease from recurring.

Long ago, we thought that ash caused urinary blockages in cats. The blame went to magnesium, and finally we settled on the composition on the urine. The key, as we now know, is the water intake of the cat. More water, less crystal formation, and a lessened chance of creating a blockage.

Constipation

This may seem like a strange thing to bring up here, but it is a serious problem in older cats. In this case, the muscles of the large intestine, which is also called the colon, are failing. The muscles can't push the fecal material through so it accumulates in the colon.

The main function of the colon is to draw water out of the feces. With the material sitting in there for a prolonged time, the result is a large lump of dried out fecal material. This is even harder to push out, so the cat becomes completely constipated and can't have a bowel movement.

You can probably guess what you'd see in this circumstance. The litter box would have no feces in it. It takes several days for these cats to become ill, but this condition needs prompt treatment with intravenous fluids and enemas.

Thromboembolism

Some people call this a kitty stroke. It is due to a heart problem where a clot forms in the upper heart chamber called the atrium. If the clot stays there, it causes no problem. But, if a small piece breaks off, it runs down an artery and plugs it.

The most common place that the clot stops is in the aorta—the large blood vessel that runs from the heart to split to the back legs. The end result is no blood to the legs. The cat immediately screams in pain as the tissues lose their oxygen supply. This lasts about one-half hour. After that, the legs are paralyzed, but the cat appears comfortable. This is how you may find the cat when you visit.

The cats that are most prone to the heart ailment that triggers this disease are large, well-fleshed males, though it is seen in females as well. In rare cases, it can cause paralysis of the left front leg.

The problem is that a thromboembolism is just a sign of an underlying heart problem. The heart will undoubtedly throw another clot and it could be fatal if it plugs a vessel in the heart or lungs.

Toxoplasmosis

While we are talking about cats, I need to mention toxoplasmosis. There is a lot of confusion about this protozoan parasite (one-celled microscopic organism).

Toxo is a zoonotic disease, which means it is passed from animals to people. It is a concern to pregnant women and people with compromised immune systems.

Cats are the natural host for toxo—it completes its life cycle in cats only. Cats pick up toxo cysts by eating contaminated meat. This can be meat we supply to our feline friends, or food they consume while hunting.

Once eaten, toxo multiplies in the cat's intestine and sheds cysts in the stool. The shedding continues for up to three weeks, but it stops once the cat's immune system mounts a response and kills the organism. Cats with toxo infections are rarely sick.

People contract toxo if they eat an infective cyst. Undercooked meat is the most common source. Think of making hamburgers and innocently licking your finger. Cat stool also poses a small risk. People can pick up toxo cysts by handling a cat, cleaning the litter box, or consuming unwashed vegetables grown in soil that cats use for toileting.

Because the organism is so common in meat, most people are exposed to toxo at some time in their lives. The problem is this—women who have not been exposed to it can suffer serious consequences if they are infected during pregnancy. The baby can suffer from a mild rash, mental retardation and loss of hearing, and possibly die from it. The mother is unaffected. Of the four million babies born in the US each year, about 3,000 are born infected with toxo.

People who have a deficient immune system—people with AIDS or those being treated with anti-rejection drugs after organ transplants—are also at risk for contracting toxo.

Toxo infections can be prevented by cooking meat (this kills toxo cysts) and washing hands if you've handled raw meat. Lastly, and this is the reason I bring this up, you want to reduce your exposure to toxo from cats if you are of a child-bearing age. Wear gloves when you change the kitty litter, or better yet, get someone else to clean the box.

The other safeguard is to have yourself tested and see if you have antibodies to toxo. If you do, you can't pick it up and your unborn child is safe. If you are not pregnant, toxo poses no threat to you.

Asthma

You've likely seen people with asthma—they breathe very hard, trying to get air in and out of the lungs. Cats suffer from the same disease. It causes labored breathing, and you see the belly working hard to move the air.

However, cats with asthma don't develop symptoms in minutes like a person does. They develop over hours or days and it lasts for days. If its severe, they can die.

Abscesses

A common affliction in cats that fight is an abscess. When cats fight, their nails and teeth penetrate the skin of their opponent. This introduces bacteria below the skin surface. These bacteria multiply and we end up with pus building up beneath the skin in the subcutaneous tissue. The skin overlying the abscess loses its blood supply. Once it is dead, it opens up and the pus drains out.

As an abscess forms, the cat likely did not feel too good because of the toxins produced by the bacteria. However, once it drains, the source of the toxins (or at least the majority of it) is gone. Though it looks dramatic, the emergency is over. An abscess can wait until the next day as long as the cat is feeling okay and eating. If not, antibiotics and surgery may be needed.

Laryngeal Spasms

We talked about reverse sneezing in dogs. Cats have their own unique breathing disorder.

The larynx is also called the voicebox. It is the hard lump you can feel at the top of your neck. Folds of tissue (laryngeal folds) close the larynx when you swallow, stopping food and water going down the airway.

Unfortunately in cats, the laryngeal folds can suddenly close and spasm shut, impeding breathing. This can be triggered by hair that the cat has licked off her body, but it may seem to occur for no reason at all. When this happens, the cat hunches up on the floor, extends the neck, often puts the tongue out, and tries to breathe through the constricted larynx. It sounds like someone is holding the throat closed.

The good news, however, is that the larynx relaxes and breathing normalizes after about 10 to 15 seconds. This is not life-threatening and the cat is totally normal between episodes. This is in contrast to asthma where the symptoms do not go away that fast.

Hair Balls

So, what is a hairball? It is a mass of matted hair in the stomach. This is quite separate from the single hairs that tickle the larynx and cause laryngeal spasms. Hair balls build up over time and they are obviously more common in long-haired cats.

The main symptom of a hair ball is vomiting, usually when the stomach is empty. It occurs then because the stomach lining closes on the hair, becoming irritated and triggering vomiting.

Assuming the cat doesn't vomit the hair ball, we treat it by getting the hair ball to pass. This is done by giving the cat a laxative. This comes in tubes, and for it to work properly, about one-quarter of the tube should be given. This lubricates the hair ball and allows it to pass through the intestine.

How do we prevent hairballs? Brush the cat and remove as much hair as you can. The other way is to give a small dose of laxative every second day or so and get the hair that is present to pass out of the stomach.

# Behavior Issues

## How to Protect Yourself from Dogs

The dogs you are going to be looking after are normally going to be very friendly. But, occasionally, you are going to find a dog that is a danger to you. Let's look at how to protect yourself.

Some dogs are extremely dominant, what we call alpha dogs, the leaders of the pack. Watch the dog when you go in the home. Does he walk through the door ahead of the owner? Does he walk around the room like he owns it? This is a dominant dog in this setting.

If he comes in with head down, tail down, and "skulking" across the floor, this is a submissive dog. Then there are the ones that just want to see you and get petted. These are the great ones to deal with.

Some submissive dogs can fool you with their submissive grin, showing all their teeth. These are nice dogs, so don't worry. You can tell the difference between an aggressive dog and one that smiles. Aggressive dogs only reveal the teeth at the very front of their mouths. When submissive dogs smile, the lip goes up high enough to show all the teeth.

Always wait and see what the dog is trying to tell you so you are not taken by surprise. A growl is an obvious message from a dog, but you can get more information from his body language. Is the hair on the back up and showing stress? Are the eyes becoming dilated to suggest he's getting scared? Does he look like he might attack?

Some owners supply muzzles. This is used if you want to do something the dog doesn't like. Also, in some areas, certain breeds (such as Put Bulls) must be muzzled if they go out on the street.

Muzzles are usually made of nylon fabric with a web buckle behind the ears. The wider part of the muzzle is put under the lower jaw. If you are unsure on how to put one on, and how to do it safely, either practice or get your friendly veterinary hospital to show you how to use one.

I'm often asked if dogs can breathe with a muzzle on. Dogs breathe through their noses, so yes, they can. The only time you might run into a problem is when a muzzle is put on a short-nosed dog that has trouble breathing even on his best days. Think Pugs and Boxers. If you have a muzzle on one of these dogs and the dog is in distress, remove it immediately.

Basket muzzles made of wire or plastic are secured behind the ears with a buckle. The dog can pant so they can be left on for a long time. They are useful for short-nosed dogs with breathing difficulties. These are often seen on aggressive dogs that are taken out in public.

## The Dangerous Dog

A dangerous dog is one that shows all the dominant gestures and appears poised to attack. I was in such a predicament when I was in veterinary college. I went into a dog's run to feed him. I went to the end of the 15 foot run to retrieve his dog bowl. As I bent down to pick it up, I heard a deep, ground-vibrating growl.

Picture this. I was at the end of a four-foot wide chain-link run complete with a wire ceiling, and a 130 pound Akita guarding my exit. I was also alone. No one was in the room because I had gone in early for my chores. My life flashed before my eyes. Well, maybe that's not quite true, but you get the idea.

So, if you get cornered by a vicious dog, what should you do? Obviously, if you can, don't put yourself in this position. Use your skills to interpret your dogs and avoid this situation.

If you do get yourself into a dangerous position, your goal is to simply get out of it. There have been cases where sitters have entered the house and the dog won't let them out. One thing many pet sitters do is get the name and number of someone who can control the dog. And, while you are stuck in the bathroom, call that person to help you out. Or, call a friend.

When you are face-to-face with an aggressive dog, avoid eye contact and don't make any quick movements. He could take that as a threat and react. Try to control your emotions and energy so that you exude the attitude that you are not afraid and you don't mean the dog harm.

Watch the dog's energy level. He is likely on high alert to start with. Keep watching. If you see him go down in level, such as stopping barking and growling to smelling the air to get your scent, that is the time for you to move slowly.

Just holding something can give you a psychological advantage. Think of a shepherd and his staff. A broom, pillow, or chair can work. You want it to block the dog or herd him. Don't use it as a weapon to threaten the dog waving it at him - that can trigger aggression. But, do use an object with confidence - if you use it in fear, the dog will know. Think of it as an extension of your arm.

A way to tell if the dog is bluffing is to see if he moves back as you advance on him. If he backs away, chances are you won't get bit unless you threaten him. On the other hand, if the dog continues to move forward, wait for his aggressive energy level to fall. Take your time.

You are probably wondering what I did with the Akita. I picked up the stainless bowl and put it between me and the jaws of death as I slowly shimmied past him. It worked. I could have also stood there or sat down and waited it out.

## The Fickle Feline

If you go into the house and the relaxed cat comes to greet you, rubbing on your legs with no threatening gestures, this is a cat you can trust. However, if she's cowering in a corner or under the couch, that's different. This cat usually does one of two things—either she runs away or she lunges for you.

Look at the ears. If they are lying flat against her head, she is probably mad. Proceed with all caution. The same holds true if the hair along the spine is raised, or she is looking directly at you. Cats with nice intents often won't look at you.

If all you have to do is feed the cat, check on things and leave, you don't need to touch her and risk an assault. But, what if you need to do something to the cat and get hold of her?

I find the best way to approach a cat is from behind her. If the cat is friendly, slide a hand under the chest and pick her up. Just a note on holding cats. Do not lift her so high that the teeth and front paws are within striking distance of your face. Some cats panic with such close contact and you can get hurt.

If you think a cat has questionable motives, once your hand gets close, go to the top of the neck and shoulders and grab the skin. This can be done fast or slowly depending on your skill and the mood of the cat. In this maneuver, you are grasping what we call the scruff. The procedure is called scruffing, and it is an effective, safe way to restrain a cat.

Interestingly, some people think that holding cats by the scruff is cruel. It isn't. Cats don't feel any pain with this hold, and they actually become relaxed when you do it. I think this goes back to when the cat was a kitten. The mother would pick them up this way and their response was to relax and not struggle.

When you do scruff a cat, get as much skin as you can. If you just get a small pinch, the cat can turn around while you are holding him and attack your hand.

Once you have hold, put the cat into a kennel or slide your hand underneath the belly to support the weight. If the cat is struggling, I just hold the scruff and lift it that way.

Here's a tip that may save you from a bad scratch, and it's simple. While you have the cat held, and before you have done anything to upset him, trim his nails. Taking the points off the nails can mean the difference between a scratch and a puncture.

Another thing I do is put an Elizabethan collar on vicious cats when I want to do anything with them (like cut nails). It stops their teeth from getting anywhere near me.

Another option is to throw a blanket, hopefully a large thick one, over the cat. You then grasp the blanket with the cat inside. You should be able to feel where the head (and teeth) is and keep your fingers away from that end. Once you have the cat controlled, put her in a carrier, blanket and all.

A pillowcase is also a great cat restraint tool. You can use it to scoop up the cat and, voila, you have an instant cat carrier! Cats tend to relax in a pillowcase and you are safe.

## Feline Wounds

You probably know this, but cats can hurt you in two different ways. One is their teeth. The other is their claws. Some of the best (or I guess, worst) injuries I have incurred as a veterinarian are from cats.

All cat wounds, especially deep ones, are painful. But, when their bacteria-laden teeth introduce an infection, they are really sore. Those wounds are swollen and red. If you see this happening, see your doctor.

There is one infection I should tell you about - Cat Scratch Fever (CSF). If you are searching your memory banks, there is a song by Ted Nugent with that name. But CSF is a human disease caused by the bacterium Bartonella. It can be transmitted by both cat bites and scratches. Because it is a disease transferable to humans, it is called a zoonosis.

This bacterial infection causes a red area at the site of the inflicted wound. Weakness, vomiting, poor appetite, and weight loss are later signs. This peculiar infection can also affect the nervous system causing prolonged, debilitating illness.

CSF is surprisingly common and it is serious. There are more than 25,000 cases each year in the United States, and about 2,000 of them require hospitalization. It does not cause illness in the cat carrying the bacterium.

# Cat Behavior Solutions

## Feline Housesoiling

When people have cats, they tend to have more than one. They also tend to keep them inside. These multi-cat households are arenas for behavioral problems. Though some individual cats can form significant relationships with other cats, the presence of other felines in the house, or even in the neighborhood, can be stressful.

Housesoiling is the number one problem in cats and is responsible for the relinquishment (rehoming or euthanasia) of many cats.

Here's a situation. You are pet sitting a client's two cats. One is a two-year-old female (spayed) that the owner adopted two months ago and the other is a four-year old neutered male who's been in the home ever since he was a kitten. Up to a few months ago, he was the only cat. He started marking (urinating) on the corner of the couch. This housesoiling is upsetting the owner. She asks if you have any advice.

The first thing you have to decide is if the cat is urinating or spraying (marking). In the case of spraying, the cat backs up to an object and marks (usually) a vertical surface. He holds the tail upright and the tip quivers. In contrast, urination is usually on a horizontal surface and the cat squats to do it. The tail is normally kept down. Also, elimination usually occurs in quiet secluded areas while marking is in plain view (that's the point of it).

These distinctions are not absolute as you can have a cat that urinates on vertical surfaces or marks on horizontal ones. And just to break a myth, both males and females can spray. Males just tend to do it more often.

In the case at hand, the cat is using the corner of a couch which is vertical. The other big clue here is that a new cat came into the house. Similar circumstances occur when an outside cat is hanging around the house (in the cat's territory). The way I think about this is the indoor cat is trying to tell the threatening cat to go away by saying "this is my home".

But, sometimes it's a problem with the litter box. Some cats are extremely fastidious and won't use a dirty box. But, there is more to it than that. Many people don't give litter boxes much thought until their cats stop using them.

The most common cause of housesoiling is an inappropriate litter box, either it's not clean enough or not the right style. It may have the wrong litter or be situated in the wrong place.

When the litter box is dirty, the cat seeks out a cleaner place to urinate or defecate—often the carpet or the bed. Litter boxes should be scooped at least daily and washed weekly with mild dish detergent (soap that rinses off easily and does not leave a lingering scent).

Litter boxes come in many forms. Most cats prefer large, uncovered litter boxes because they can get in them and turn around easier. If your cat likes to scatter litter when digging the right hole, high sides can help confine the mess. If your cat is old (arthritic) or small, his box should have low sides. In fact, if you see an old cat that has never had problems start missing the box, suggest an examination. The cat could be in pain. In these old kitties, I get the owner to cut down one side of the liter box to allow an easier entry.

Covered litter boxes keep the litter out of sight but they also trap odors. If you want to use one of these boxes, you must keep it exceptionally clean. I usually get the owner to remove the lid and just use the bottom half.

Most cats prefer fine-grained unscented litters. Scoopable litters that clump have the advantage of being easy to clean, but if a cat urinates a large amount (has kidney problem), the feet may get wet and litter material may stick to the hair between the pads of their feet.

Scented litters may be attractive for people, but they may repel some cats. If you keep the litter box clean, you won't need deodorants to keep the area smelling fresh.

Some people have good success with wood pellets for litter. This product is absorbent and can be composted in the garden. They key is this - once you find a litter your cat likes, don't change it. If you want to try a new litter, give your cat a choice - one box with his regular litter and one with the new product.

Your cat needs privacy when toileting so his litter box should be in a quiet yet accessible location where pets and people can't sneak up on him. Don't put it out in the open or in a busy hallway. You need to have at least one litter box per cat in your home. Experts tell us it should be the number of cats plus one. If you have a multi-level home, you should have a box on each floor. A convenient box is a well used box.

Now that we have the basics on litter boxes, let's go back to our case and solve it.

He may be upset because the owner added a second cat or he might be marking because the owner let the litter box get dirty. Also, how many litter boxes are present? There should be three in this house. This is the first thing I'd do if there is only one box.

Now we look at what to do about the couch. It needs cleaning but don't use ammonia or chlorine (bleach) as they can produce a scent that confuses the cat. Clean with a feline odor and stain remover/neutralizer or a washing powder followed by rubbing alcohol. Wait until it's dry before the cat has access to the area again.

Next, we remove the triggers for the marking (if we can). In this case, if we assume it is due to the new cat, we could try and decrease the tension between them. Adding extra litter boxes may help if he is stressed by having just one box. We'll look at more ideas in the next section on inter-cat relationships.

You can also get the cat thinking differently about the function of the place he has chosen to mark. You could put a litterbox there, or even the food and water bowls. Some people put physical barriers in place. If the cat is urinating on a bed, close the bedroom door.

If the cat is climbing on the counter, putting a sheet of aluminum foil on the surface can deter them from jumping up. It seems to feel bad on their feet.

Make sure that the owner is not punishing the cat. This creates more problems than it cures. You may find that the cat then marks in hidden and hard to detect places.

There are novel treatments we can add to these ideas. Pheromones are hormones that make the cat feel more at ease. One brand called "Feliway" has produced some positive results. I recommend the diffuser over the spray as it keeps a constant level in the environment. We can also look at medication to calm the cat. Both of these need to be used with behavior training.

Remember that housesoiling is only a symptom. You still need to find the cause and address it.

## Inter-Cat Aggression

When two cats meet, they don't give each other a hug. Their communication aims to keep distance between them. Their postures and vocalizing are meant to scare the other cat away. They also urinate on objects and put their scent on things to tell other cats to leave their territory.

Also, and this is a misunderstood fact for most people, the goal for a cat is self-preservation. They think of themselves and not other cats. They do not take turns eating food like dogs do in the pack structure with the dominant ones eating first and the submissive ones taking the leftovers. There is no such thing as submission in cat-to-cat and cat-to-human interactions. The dominance theories we have for dogs don't apply.

When dogs get together, their posturing often stops overt attacks before they get going. Cats continue to the fight. And, unlike dogs, they don't have to repair relationships for survival.

Also, cats are able to exist in a social vacuum. Though they may tolerate or possibly enjoy interactions with people or other cats, they don't need it.

If we look at the dynamics of several cats in a house, it is complex. Two cats may form a social group but another is exterior to it. As well, one cat may create an alliance with two individual cats even though those two cats can't get along.

Cats in natural settings do not share resources, but we expect them to do this in multi-cat households. This includes resting places, watering holes, and feeding stations. We may think they get along because they all come together to eat. But, because food is a vital resource, they suppress their behaviors. For a short time, they suspend hostility, but this strains the relationship even further. You can tell this is happening by asking a question—where do the cats congregate? Owners often tell you that the cats do not share the same room at all except at feeding times.

To reduce the tension, feed the cats in different rooms. If they have sub-groups, you could feed those together, but many prefer to eat alone given the chance.

The same holds true with water. Put several bowls of water around the house so that they can drink away from other cats. Litter boxes, I think, you already know about. Spread them about the house, not in the same room. Provide elevated resting places, as well as retreats, and enough of them for the cats to separate. Lastly, exercise (play) can also help decrease tension between cats by reducing nervous energy.

# Dog Behavior Solutions

## Submissive Behavior

When you enter the house, a submissive dog may come up to you, cowering, and he might even urinate on the floor. Worse, he may hide under the bed and you can't get near him to let him out to the bathroom. Or, once you let him out, herding may be the only way to get him back inside. You can help these dogs, but it takes time. You need to look at how to change your interaction.

First, what you shouldn't do. Don't yell at the dog. Don't punish him like pulling him outside or hitting him for urinating. Dominating a dog like this just makes it worse and destroys the relationship you are trying to forge.

So, how can we change the behavior of a submissive dog? Start by ignoring the dog. Imagine he's not there. This is what he wants—

he wants to disappear. Once he's figured out you mean no harm, let him come to you. Don't force him.

Sit on the floor with your back to the dog, and allow the dog (mainly his nose) to check you out. You must exude calmness for him to do this. Make yourself small. Standing in front of a submissive dog with a hand out is scary to him.

Once the dog is comfortable being close to you, you can then offer treats or extend a hand. Don't lift your hand up too high; keep it low. Always pet underneath so that you are not showing dominance. Petting a dog from above can push him into submission again.

For some dogs, it may take weeks before they will let you touch them. And, going too fast will just set you back. Don't offer treats until you have gained the dog's trust. The dog's desire for food may force him to be too forward and push his comfort zone.

Once you have gained confidence, you can then get bigger (crouch or sit on a chair). Over time, your dog will accept more and more interaction. You may even be able to stand next to him. Many people don't realize how dominant this is.

If you have a dog hiding in a kennel or behind the couch, don't nurture the fear by petting or sharing affection. Let him stay where he is until he is ready to come out for hunger or inquisitiveness.

Don't rush the physical affection. Remember that petting is for your sake, not the dog's. You may feel sorry and want to assure him, but just do it from a distance and let him determine if he wants to be touched.

There can be a negative side to submissive dogs. If you are too pushy, you may scare the dog so much that he may bite. This is fear aggression. Watch the dog. If you see fear in his eyes, take it as a signal and back off before you push him too far.

## Overexuberant Behavior

Why is a dog exuberant? The core reason is that people have let him do that and they bring his energy up rather than bring it down. They've encouraged the behavior.

I see this daily at my hospital. The dog is bouncing off the walls and owner is trying to calm him by yelling "Buddy, relax." As a trainer friend of mine says, "don't add spice to an already spicy soup." Mirroring the dog's energy keeps it going.

So what can you do when you arrive and the dog is crazy? Like the submissive dog, start by ignoring the dog. Eye contact or sound will only add energy to the dog's boisterous behavior. Don't let his behavior get a response from you.

Once he's settled down and is not all over you, you can go to the next stage. Move the dog to a rest/relaxation area and ask for a sit-stay or a downstay. It may take many times to get the dog to stay, but continue. You need to win this psychological battle. Do it calmly to relax the dog. Don't get upset.

Once you've reached that stage, you can now get ready for a walk or some exercise. Only when the dog is calm can you share affection. But, rather than exciting the dog with touch, food is a good idea at this point (as long as he is not extremely food motivated).

Exuberant dogs often get in that state because they lack physical and psychological challenge. A tired dog is a well behaved dog.

You can walk, run, rollerblade, and even ride a bike with these dogs. Some dogs do well on treadmills with minimal training. Just start slow so you don't scare them.

Of course, as a pet sitter, you will likely be dealing with an exuberant dog each time you visit and the possibilities for training may seem minimal with the time constraints you have. Hopefully, you can get the dog on his way and tell the owner how to help the situation. It may end in you being employed to exercise the dog!

# Excessive Barking

Let's start with why a dog barks. It may be because his environment is boring. He has nothing to do. He might have too much energy and nothing to expend it on. Part of this is that he needs a job and suffers without one. Also, he may be left alone for extended times and be dealing with separation anxiety.

Though fear is another reason for barking, he may also have been trained to bark, alerting the owner to intruders. In these cases, you can use the same signal that you used for the exuberant dog to get his attention and then praise him for staying quiet.

If you arrive and the dog is barking, you can quickly train him not to bark. Put a toy or ball in his mouth and say "No Noise". Follow with verbal praise or a reward for stopping barking. The dog will learn that there is something positive if he stops barking.

The first thing is to exercise the body and the mind of the dog. This means going for walks, but if you can arrange some off-leash time, it is even better. Do some training while you are on the walk so that the dog has to think rather than plod beside you. Agility classes are trying both physically and mentally as the dog has to think as well. You can also train dogs to use a treadmill. It takes concentration and burns off nervous energy.

If the dog barks when you leave, pretend to leave and when he barks, come back abruptly with a "no noise" command and send him to a rest area for a sitstay or downstay. Eventually, you will get a little time without barking. Even if it's only 30 seconds, step back in and reward the dog for not barking. You can then increase the time and he will eventually give up barking and wait for the positive reinforcement.

If it is people that he barks at, get someone to walk by, but not close enough to incite a bark. Get the dog to sitstay and reward him for being quiet. Get the person to walk closer and continue the praise for quietness.

A difficult to treat situation is barking due to separation anxiety, mainly because you are not there. I've got a few ideas for this.

Provide a scent item. Give the dog a soft object that smells like you. You can also wear a t-shirt to bed and each morning, give it to the dog as you leave. Of course, a new shirt every night.

Play soothing music. This can help drown out exterior noises that may sensitize the dog to bark.

Reduce presence and absence contrast. For 20 minutes before you leave and after you arrive, completely ignore the dog. No eye contact, speaking, or fast, noisy activity. You want the dog to think that there is no difference between you being there and not being there.

Consistent routine. Keep feeding times, bathroom breaks, play times and walks at routine times. Structure means stability.

The last resort (in my mind) is an anti-bark collar. I do not recommend an electric shock collar. Some dogs will endure the pain yet keep barking. They have a low success rate. The alternative is a citronella collar that sprays a "lemon" solution into the dog's face when he barks. These do not cause pain and have an almost 90 percent success rate. However, some dogs don't seem to mind the smell and others can figure out when the reservoir is empty and they continue to bark.

The key with barking is to not reward any inappropriate behavior. You can't be trying to curtail barking yet rewarding the dog when he barks at strangers.

Is debarking surgery a suitable solution to training for stopping barking? This is a modification of the dog's vocal chords. It seldom complete eliminates a dog's bark. The volume of the bark substantially decreases, but most dogs learn to bark. It is a very contentious issue. Some say it is a last-resort for incessant barkers. Others say it is cruel and unnecessary.

The surgery does not address the underlying reasons for the dog's constant barking. The dog's life is unchanged. I think we can help these dogs using behavior, if the owners are willing to put the time and effort into it.

# Pet First Aid and Emergencies

By their nature, emergencies are never planned, and they always seem to happen at the worst time. They range in severity from inconsequential to life-threatening. They can be due to unexpected allergic reactions, poisonings, burns, electrical shocks, or trauma. It is up to you to determine if you need immediate veterinary assistance.

I want you to know what can go wrong with animals under your care and what to do when it does. Suppose you arrive at the house and the dog has a mad run around the back yard and cuts its paw on a piece of glass, do you know what to do? What if the cat jumps on a hot stove? If the dog is bitten by a wasp and its muzzle swells, what's the next step? These are all things you should know how to handle. Let's look at things you are likely to see.

Bleeding

You may have a pet that's cut itself or has been bitten. In all these cases, the pet should be examined by a veterinarian, but you should try to control the bleeding first, if you can. There are two reasons for doing this. One is that you don't want the pet losing blood. The other is a practical reason. You don't want the blood all over your car. If you put the cat or small dog in a carrier, it won't matter as much.

If the bleeding is severe, apply direct pressure to the bleeding area using a compress (a facecloth, sanitary napkin, or gauze pad). You can hold it on with your hand or bandage it in place. Once blood starts to clot, do not pull off the bandage to check. This disturbs the clot and gets it bleeding again. If blood soaks through the compress, simply add another on top.

Do you know the difference between arterial and venous blood? When an artery bleeds, you see bright red blood pumping from the wound. Venous blood is darker and just seeps; you won't see a pulse. A pet can lose much more blood from an artery than a vein.

In the case of a cut artery on a leg, you can reduce the blood loss by applying pressure to the main artery supplying the limb. For rear leg bleeding, pressure is applied to the femoral artery, and for front leg bleeding, the brachial artery. Both of these arteries course down the inside surface of the leg. Apply pressure on the artery as high as possible, close to the body.

If bleeding is life-threatening, a tourniquet can be applied, but it should be reserved for a limb that is not expected to be saved. This occurred in a dog I saw who literally got his leg cut off by a train. It was a horrible accident, but his owner, who I still admire for what he did, took his belt off and cinched it around the bleeding stump that was left. He saved the dog's life.

The official way to put on a tourniquet is to wind a wide piece of cloth loosely around around the leg and knot it. A stick or similar object is put under the loop and twisted until the cloth tightens on the leg.

It's turned enough to stop the bleeding. If the limb is to be saved, the tourniquet must be loosened every five minutes for a two minute interval to allow some blood flow to the tissue. Left on, the tissue will die. If the bleeding is this severe, you should be on your way to the veterinary hospital right away.

If you want to get bleeding controlled, begin by covering the wound with gauze, one of the compresses mentioned earlier, or a bandage pad. This is held in place with gauze wrapped loosely around the leg. Cover this with adhesive bandage material. It should cover the gauze and the area above and below it. Once it sticks to the hair, it will stay on.

Once the wound is protected, take the pet to the veterinarian to complete treatment. It may require continued bandaging and antibiotic therapy, or suturing.

Burns

Burns occasionally happen in pets. The most common way is for a cat to jump on a hot range or wood stove. If you are pet sitting, it's unlikely there will be a stove on while the owners are away, but if you are there for a mid-day check, you might see a cat with a sore foot.

If you happen to see a burn occur, apply a cold wet compress to the site for at least 30 minutes. Change the compress frequently to ensure it is always cool.

However, it's more likely you'll see the result of a burn. We see this as blisters on the pads on one or more feet. In all cases, seek veterinary help.

Allergic Reactions

Allergic reactions are most commonly initiated by insect bites, but can occasionally be induced by vaccinations, medications, or foods. Reactions to injected allergens, such as bee stings and vaccines, can range from mild to life-threatening. The worst reactions, which occur within minutes of the injection, stimulate edematous swelling (fluid build-up) in the larynx (throat) which obstructs breathing. It can also send the pet into shock. I'll go over shock shortly, but even though these reactions can be rapidly fatal, they are thankfully very rare.

The allergic reaction I see most often is swelling of the face (called angioneurotic edema). The lips, eyelids, and sometimes ear flaps will thicken so much that even a Dachshund can look like a Shar Pei. If you see this reaction, don't hit the alarm button. Facial edema is usually evident 30 minutes to six hours after the insect bite and the good news - by then it's too late for either of the fatal reactions to occur.

I saw my sleeping dog Courtney get bitten by a mosquito on the nose. She didn't wake up. Half an hour later (she's still sleeping), her muzzle and eyelids started to swell. She finally woke up with a horribly swollen, itchy nose. This shows you how fast this can occur. And, in many allergic reactions, you never know the reason it occurred.

The last symptom of an allergic response is hives, technically known as urticaria. Though hives are easy to see on short-haired dogs, the bumps may not be evident if your companion has a thick coat. Even if you can't see them, you will know hives are there because your friend will be extremely itchy all over.

Allergic reactions are treated according to their severity. The first two reactions (shock or laryngeal edema) are emergency situations needing immediate veterinary help. If a dog has suffered any of these reactions, owners usually carry an injection of epinephrine (a bee kit) wherever the dog goes. Milder allergic reactions are treated with antihistamines and possibly corticosteroids.

## Shock

Shock is a nebulous term. The dictionary defines it as a state of profound depression of the vital processes associated with reduced blood volume and pressure. The practical way I look at shock is that it is triggered by a severe drop in blood pressure. Causes include extreme blood loss, severe dehydration, allergic reactions which cause blood pooling in internal organs, toxins, and even intense pain.

When blood pressure first starts to fall, the body responds by speeding up the heart so that more blood is pumped. Next, the blood vessels supplying the extremities (feet and ears) constrict so that blood is shunted to the vital organs.

There are two important signs of shock that you can recognize in your companion at home. The first is a change in pulse. It changes to rapid and weak.

The second important sign of shock is a pale gum color. Body temperature also falls. In later stages, weakness and depression develop. Untreated, severe shock is fatal. The brain and heart don't get enough blood to function adequately.

The first step in shock treatment is to recognize it. If you can, keep the pet warm. Just wrap the dog or cat with blankets. The last step is to get to the hospital as fast as you can.

As you can see, your role in shock isn't treating it. I want you to be able to detect it and act appropriately, hopefully saving a life.

## Vomiting and Diarrhea

I see patients almost every day that come in with the complaint of a sudden onset of vomiting and diarrhea. Many of these are mild cases and attributed to "dietary indiscretion" or "garbage gastritis". This usually occurs in dogs that eat something that's bad. In cats, hair balls are a more common culprit of vomiting.

However, symptoms like vomiting and diarrhea are not always benign. Other causes are parvoviral infections, intestinal blockages, or pancreatitis, the latter being triggered by meals of high-fat foods. These can all be life-threatening.

A dog with vomiting and diarrhea can be treated at home if he is not depressed and if the symptoms are mild. The best approach is to withhold food and water for at least 12 hours. If the symptoms abate, offer water, then bland food such as white rice with a little added cooked chicken. As long as the vomiting or diarrhea does not resume, the dog's regular diet can then be slowly introduced.

When cats are vomiting, I consider that more serious. I'd get them checked unless they are still feeling good and eating.

If there is blood in the pet's stool or vomitus (what they vomit), if the pet becomes dehydrated, or if he is depressed, veterinary help should be sought. Even though they may not look ill, puppies under 16 weeks of age and geriatric dogs or cats are a special case. They should always receive veterinary care if vomiting or diarrhea continues for more than 12 hours with no signs of abatement. This is because these individuals are prone to dehydration.

Foreign Bodies

Dogs and foreign objects seem to attract each other. Sticks can get lodged between the upper teeth across the palate causing dogs to frantically paw at their mouth. These objects can be removed with a strong finger grip or a pair of pliers, as long as you have a compliant dog.

Barbed fish hooks that pierce the tongue, cheek, or any part of the body need to be pushed through the tissue in order to be removed. Some dogs need an anesthetic to resolve this painful problem, especially when multi-pronged hooks are lodged in the mouth. You're probably wondering why a dog would eat a hook. It's because there may be a little tasty bait on it or it smells good.

Dogs can swallow just about anything, and luckily, most of them will eventually pass through the intestines. If a dog is observed in the act of eating a foreign object, watch him closely for signs of vomiting, depression, inappetance, or dehydration. If the dog exhibits no symptoms, just watch his stool carefully for the object to appear. It may take several days to pass.

If symptoms do appear, the object may be causing a blockage in the gastrointestinal tract. Veterinary assistance is needed. He or she will take radiographs. Foreign bodies such as stones are easy to see because they are so dense. If something is found, it's time for surgery to remove it.

Eye Problems

When a pet has an eye problem, no matter what kind, the impulse is to rub. Damage from self-mutilation can sometimes be worse than the original problem. If a dog has red eyes, is squinting, or has a lot of tearing and discharge, he should be fitted with an Elizabethan collar (you should have one in the first aid kit) to prevent rubbing his eye.

If an "E-collar" isn't available, a piece of cardboard can be fashioned into a collar for small dogs. For larger dogs, a plastic bucket with the bottom cut out can be placed over the dog's head. It won't be pretty, but it is functional.

All eye problems should be treated as emergency situations, meaning the dog should be assessed by a veterinarian as soon as possible. Small exophthalmic breeds such as Pugs and Pekingese are at risk for having an eye pop out of its socket. If this happens, place a clean wet towel over the eye to safeguard it while you transport the dog to a veterinarian.

Bloat

People who own large, deep-chested dogs should be aware of gastric dilatation-volvulus, commonly called bloat. This disease can kill within hours of the first signs of distress.

The symptoms of bloat include drooling, retching or attempting to vomit, anxiety, restlessness, and pacing. The abdomen may feel or look distended (bloated). In just a short time, the dog can go into shock and die. Bloat requires immediate veterinary attention. The longer the delay, the less likely it is the dog will survive.

Whelping Problems

Chances are, you won't be pet sitting a pregnant dog, but it's good to know this information. As whelping time approaches, the bitch's mammary glands engorge with milk and she starts to exhibit nesting behaviour, grabbing a toy and hiding in a closet. About 24 hours before she starts labour, her temperature drops about one degree Celsius (two degrees Fahrenheit). This is how breeders monitor time for birthing. At delivery time, her mucous vaginal discharge changes to a greenish colour. A brown or foul-smelling discharge means something is wrong.

Prolonged labour is always a concern. Once a bitch is having visible contractions, she should deliver her first puppy within a half hour (some veterinarians say one hour). There should always be progressive (outward) movement of the puppy through the birth canal. If there is no puppy showing, or it is not moving, the bitch needs assistance.

Cats are really no different in what to look for, but they rarely have problems. A female cat is called a queen and the birthing process is called queening.

Preventive Medicine

Many emergencies can be prevented. Diseases can be detected in the early stages before they become critical. Heart and kidney failure as well as diabetes are examples of ailments that can be readily managed IF they are discovered before they become an emergency.

All pet sitters should purchase and read a good pet first aid book. This reference will not only act as a guide in the event of an emergency, it will also help determine when homecare or immediate veterinary intervention is needed.

Pet sitters are invaluable in preventive medicine. If you can see a problem—any problem—alert the owner so they can act on it.

# Cardiopulmonary Resuscitation (CPR)

Cardiopulmonary Arrest - Sudden cessation of heart and lung function (the pumping of blood and air exchange)

There are many reasons for cardiopulmonary arrest. In pets, drowning and electrocution are two of the most likely causes. Airway obstruction from a foreign object lodged in the trachea or from throat swelling secondary to an allergic reaction can also cause cardiopulmonary arrest. Once the heart stops, you only have five minutes before irreversible brain damage occurs. Revival after this time is unlikely.

If you find a pet flat out but are unsure what happened to him, you first need to determine if he is unconscious or dead. To check him, step on his tail. If you startle a deeply sleeping animal by touching his head, you could be bitten. If there is no response, check for a pulse in one of the arteries or feel the chest. If nothing, look for breathing. If you don't see any, place your finger on the surface of the eye (the cornea). This is very painful. If there is no reaction, the brain is not functioning and he is no longer alive. If there is a response, CPR should be initiated.

When performing CPR, there are three steps to follow that are as simple as your ABCs.

A—AIRWAY

B—BREATHING

C—CIRCULATION

Let's start with dogs. If he is not breathing, start the "A" part of CPR. Ensure the airway is open by extending his head and neck and pulling his tongue forward. If there is saliva or vomit in the mouth, wipe it out. To prove his airway is open, push on the chest so you can hear or feel air come out.

The next step is to give the dog a series of test breaths. Hold the corners of the mouth closed so that air doesn't leak out. In larger dogs, pull the tongue forward between the teeth to seal the mouth. A breath is then given into the nostrils and allowed to escape. Three breaths are given and then the dog is observed for spontaneous breathing.

If the dog does not breath on his own, move to part "B". You are now breathing for the dog at a rate of 20-25 breaths per minute.

Once respirations are initiated, feel the chest for a heart beat just behind the elbow. If there is none, begin chest (or cardiac) compressions to promote circulation (part "C").

A very small dog should be laid on his side. His chest should be compressed about one inch behind his elbow, using a forefinger and thumb. The depth of the compression is two to three centimeters. A larger dog should be positioned on his back so his sternum can be compressed for a distance of three to seven centimeters.

Chest compressions should be given at a rate of 80-100 compressions per minute. When performing CPR, you can give three heart compressions followed by one compression and one breath given simultaneously. There are many different ratios published, but the idea is to keep the blood moving and get fresh into the lungs.

Feline CPR is the same as in small dogs. Lie them on their side and compress the heart just behind the elbow. The key with little patients is to not blow hard in the nose. You want the chest to rise, but it's not a competition to see how high you can make it go.

## Poisonings

Pets are curious creatures, so if there is a poison around, they can find it. Poisonings often have severe consequences because it is rare to actually see it consumed and treatment is often delayed. By familiarizing you with the various poisonings, you can hopefully recognize the symptoms early and possibly save the pet's life. Better yet, you might be able to prevent it from occurring.

The first sign of many intoxications is vomiting. It is the body's attempt to eliminate the poison. Some toxins cause profuse salivation and many cause depression and lethargy. Others stimulate convulsions or bleeding. Though these symptoms can be seen with a whole gamut of diseases, poisonings cause these signs to appear suddenly and unexpectedly in otherwise normal dogs.

Antifreeze (Ethylene glycol)

One of the most common and serious poisonings veterinarians see is from ethylene glycol (EG). EG is the toxic ingredient in most automobile antifreeze solutions. It is very sweet tasting and pets are attracted to it. Once swallowed, it is rapidly absorbed and metabolized. EG causes acute kidney failure.

Within a few hours of EG ingestion, the pet becomes weak and staggers as if "drunk". Most vomit. Over a few days, they start urinating a lot and become lethargic. Stupor, convulsions, coma, and death soon follow. To ensure survival, treatment should be instituted within an hour of ingestion—not an easy task if you don't see your friend consume the antifreeze.

EG poisoning can be prevented. If you see antifreeze leaking under a car, clean it up (kitty litter is a great absorbant for this). I tell my clients to have propylene glycol, a pet-friendly antifreeze, put in the car's radiator instead of EG. It is a little more expensive, but far less toxic.

Slug Bait (Metaldehyde)

Metaldehyde is the active ingredient in slug bait. This poison causes convulsions that, though dramatic, can usually be controlled with medication. I call metaldehyde a "friendly" poison—it causes no lasting damage once it is cleared from the body. This is only a hazard in wet areas where slugs abound.

## Rat Poisons

Rat poisons can be broken into two categories—those that cause neurological symptoms, and those that cause bleeding. Strychnine causes severe convulsions that paralyze respiratory muscles, causing asphyxiation. Treatment must be initiated promptly to give the pet any chance of survival.

Most rat poisons used these days inhibit blood clotting. In severe cases, bleeding, either external or internal, can be so significant that it leads to loss of blood and subsequent death. It is treated by re-establishing clotting ability by administering vitamin K by injection.

## Chocolate

Chocolate toxicity is primarily a dog problem because cats don't seem to crave this delicacy. We see this occur around Christmas time when chocolates are left in a bowl or the dog finds wrapped chocolate under the tree.

Most of you know that chocolate can be toxic, but do you know why? First, it contains caffeine. Though chocolate-eating hyperactive dogs pace for hours, the effect wears off. Chocolate can also cause indigestion.

But, the real poison in chocolate is theobromine. It causes muscle twitching, seizures, and possibly even death. The amount of theobromine in chocolate varies. Dark chocolate usually contains more than milk chocolate, and baker's chocolate contains even more.

## Xylitol

This artificial sweetener is used in sugar-free gums, and lots of other things destined for human consumption. Dogs are exquisitely sensitive to xylitol and just a small amount can cause blood sugar to drop to critical levels, what we call hypoglycemia. Two sticks of gum can kill a Doberman.

Fertilizers

Fertilizers are not generally toxic, usually inducing stomach upset and vomiting. Products with large amounts of nitrogen, such as fish fertilizer, can create blood problems.

Drugs and Alcohol

Recreational (illegal) drugs can also cause toxicities in pets. Marijuana causes a "high" just as it does in people. Dogs stand stockstill, stiff, and unaware of what's going on. Sedation may be required until its effect wears off. "Harder" drugs are more serious and can cause death, depending on the dose.

Alcohol is not tolerated well by dogs, partly because of their small size, but also because they are not used to consuming it. It does not take much to induce alcohol poisoning in a Chihuahua. Long term alcohol consumption can cause liver damage in dogs just as it does in people.

Petroleum Products

Petroleum products (oil, gas, or solvents) can be toxic when absorbed through the skin or when they are licked off and swallowed. Lighter consistency products such as turpentine are more likely to cause toxicity because they are rapidly absorbed. It is critical to bathe the pet immediately, using soap to break up the petroleum product. Heavier products like tar or thick oil can be diluted with a light vegetable oil before being removed with soap.

Onions

Onions, both raw and cooked, can be toxic to select dogs. They cause a hemolytic anemia (red blood cell breakdown) that can be severe enough to warrant a blood transfusion. There may be a genetic susceptibility.

Plants

Many plants are poisonous. The two most well recognized ones in dogs are Dieffenbachia and the Christmas plant, the Poinsettia. Both cause stomach upset and mouth irritation. Lilies cause kidney failure in cats. If you are unsure if a particular plant is toxic, call your local poison control centre for advice or check the links I have provided.

Poison Control Centres

These are great places. You can call them directly, but it's best if the veterinarian makes the call. I've had people call me when their (usually dogs) have scooped up and consumed a dropped medication. Though these centres are designed for people, they can likely tell you if there is a concern with the medication in animals. There are also some places that cater specifically to pets. For example, the American SPCA Animal Poison Center in Urbana, Illinois charges a consultation fee for calls.

When enlisting the help of a human poison control centre, it is best to work through your veterinarian. Because these centres are funded for human poisonings, people cases take the priority. This said, the many centres will assist if they can.

# Poisoning Protocol

• Call your veterinarian immediately. If possible, tell her what the poison is, when the poisoning may have occurred, and how much was ingested.

• Protect yourself and the pet from injury. If a pet is convulsing, clear the furniture from around him and use his hind leg or tail to pull him to the middle of the room. To carry him, put a blanket on the floor, roll him onto it and then pick it up like a hammock.

• Induce vomiting. If a dog has consumed a poison within the last two hours, vomiting may help eliminate it from the body before it is absorbed. Only do this under veterinary direction. Use hydrogen peroxide at one teaspoon for five pounds body weight. If there is any chance that the pet may have been intentionally poisoned, save the vomitus for analysis. Put it in a plastic bag in the refrigerator. It is very hard to get cats to vomit so don't try it.

• Clean the skin. If the toxin is on the skin, remove it. Use dishwashing soap to remove oils. With skunk spraying, mix one quart (approximately one liter) of household 3% hydrogen peroxide, 1/4-cup baking soda and one teaspoonful liquid soap. Wearing gloves, bathe the animal thoroughly, then rinse him well with copious amounts of warm water. The mixture can also be put into a spray bottle and applied, but make sure it does not get into the eyes. Rub it in well and then rinse it off after 15 minutes. This mixture cannot be stored; effectiveness is quickly lost.

• Get the pet to the veterinarian. As a pet sitter, it's important to get the pet evaluated. The veterinarian can continue specific treatment for the poisoning and (hopefully) prevent long-term complications.

## Home First Aid Kit for People and Pets

• Adhesive tape – For bandaging.

• Sterile dressing pads – Covers wounds (can use sanitary napkins).

• Cling gauze – Holds pads on wound.

• Gauze sponges – Covers or cleans wounds.

• Adhesive bandage – Holds bandage to skin/hair.

• Scissors – Cuts bandage material.

• Antiseptic soap – Cleans wounds.

• Antibiotic ointment – Treats minor wounds.

• Thermometer – Measures body temperature.

• Eye wash – Washes eyes.

• Hydrogen peroxide (3%) – Induces vomiting.

• Elizabethan collar – Prevents wound licking and eye rubbing.

• Blanket/towel – For warmth or transport.

• Rope leash – Restraint.

# Medicating

Diseases and conditions are treated with medications. This could be drops for an eye condition, ointment for ear disease, tablets for heart problems or arthritis, or insulin injections for a diabetic cat. If you know how to give medications, it can help you take better care of pets that need special care. As well, it can give you a boost over other pet sitters.

Subcutaneous fluids

Some pets, especially older cats, receive fluids under the skin on a regular basis because their kidneys are failing. Without the added fluids, they become dehydrated. This is a skill that you can easily learn so let's go over how to do it.

Fluids, which are salt solutions, come in a fluid bag with an intravenous line attached to it. The only thing you have to add is a new needle (for sterility purposes).

If you are using this apparatus, the fluid bag must be mounted above the cat such as on a kitchen door handle or a wire hanger over a door so that gravity keeps the fluid moving.

Grasp the skin over the shoulders. This is the place where they don't seem to feel it. With the skin tented (pulled up), insert the needle into the subcutaneous tissue. I tend to put it in next to my thumb and pointed into the skin tent rather than pointing into the cat to avoid going deep.

You can now open the valve on the intravenous line. This lets the fluid flow down the line and into the cat. Hopefully, you made a mark on the bag so that you know where to stop the fluid. I often get people to give 100 milliliters in one go.

Once you are finished, pull the needle out and cap it. You will likely see a few drops of fluid coming out of the tiny hole in the cat's skin, but don't worry about it. The bag should be stored in the refrigerator and warned up prior to the next use. I don't use a microwave because it melts the plastic in the IV line. Instead, warm the fluids by putting them in a bowl or sink filled with warm water. Just warm to take the chill off the fluids.

The other way to give fluids is with a syringe. You need to draw the fluid into the syringe first by having a needle inserted into the fluid bag. You can then inject the fluids through the same needle into the cat or through a butterfly catheter. If you do an Internet search for "SQ fluids in cats" you can see how this is done.

Insulin Injections for Diabetics

Insulin is measured in International Units (IUs). Most insulin is 100 IU per milliliter, though there is a veterinary product that is 40 IU per milliliter. There are specific syringes designed for each product. Do not mix the syringes as an overdose or underdose is possible. The needles on insulin syringes are very small and most dogs and cats do not even notice when they penetrate the skin surface.

Insulin must be mixed before withdrawing it from the bottle, but don't shake it. Vigorous shaking is thought to damage the insulin. Invert the bottle, slowly mixing it.

Insulin is always given just under the skin as a subcutaneous injection. There is one thing to always remember with insulin. If you think you messed up the injection, do not give a second one. If you got even a little insulin in and then added a full dose, you are overdosing. This can cause a potentially life-threatening hypoglycemia (low blood sugar).

This brings up the most important point with handling diabetics - how to recognize and handle hypoglycemia.

A diabetic cat I had, my own cat, was little old girl called Faith. A cute little cat, she taught me a lot about controlling diabetes. She was good most of the time, but for some unknown reason, she would suddenly decide to become hypoglycemic.

One time, we arrived home early evening. We found her flat out on the carpet, unresponsive to calling or touch. She was comatose. I couldn't even feel a pulse. We took her to my hospital thinking that it would be her last ride. Once there, I checked her blood sugar. It was so low, it wouldn't even read.

So, we gave her an injection of sugar (actually dextrose) into her vein. Within a minute she was sitting up. A minute later, she was eating. She was our miracle kitty.

If the dose of insulin is too high, the pet's blood sugar drops far too low because all the glucose moves out of the blood and into the cells. Hypoglycemia causes weakness and it can even trigger seizures, ending in death.

Because hypoglycemia is so serious, every owner (and pet sitter) of a diabetic pet on insulin must be prepared to deal with it. It is essential that they have a ready source of sugar available such as Karo syrup, icing gel, or honey. If a pet shows any signs even remotely suggestive of hypoglycemia, the sugar is given orally or rubbed on the gums to raise blood glucose. You can never be wrong doing this.

If you are giving insulin injections to a diabetic cat or dog, you need to find out:

• The dose

• Time for the injection

• Who their vet is

If you haven't given insulin before, a great way to find out how is to have a client you want to pet sit for that has a diabetic pet show you how. Of course, don't charge the client to go over and have the lesson. This will create a strong bond between you and that client and give you a skill that you can use with other clients.

The other resource for learning about injections is the internet. There are many videos showing how to give insulin injection to animals.

Oral Medications

You may be an expert in giving medication orally, but maybe you've never opened a pet's mouth to put a pill down. This part of the lesson is devoted to these latter people.

To give a pill, simply open the mouth and put the medication at the base of the tongue. That sounds easy, doesn't it? Well, not exactly. Beyond having your pet tug in the opposite direction of the hand holding the pill, you also have to combat the tongue, which is constantly working to eject anything you put on it. It can be quite a fiasco! However, I'll give you tips on how to do it.

I find the best way to open a dog's mouth is to place my hand over the dog's nose and slip my thumb behind the upper fang (canine tooth) and onto the palate (roof of the mouth). I then lift the nose up so the dog reflexively opens his mouth. I hold the medication between my opposite hand's thumb and forefinger and drop it in. Take a look at the picture below to see how I position my hands.

There are also less traumatic ways to do it. One is to wrap the pill in something tasty. This can be a little cheese, canned cat food, or a slice of roast beef. Then there's the old three-wiener trick. Cut three pieces of wiener, each one a half-inch to an inch long. Cut a slit into the second one and insert the pill, then line the three pieces up where the dog can see them. Give the first piece. The dog checks it out and figures it's safe. Give the second (pill-containing) piece, but have the third piece in front of his nose ready to go. He's so busy eating the second piece to get the third that he doesn't even notice the medication.

Another alternative is to use specially designed pill pockets sold for this purpose. These come in different flavors and sizes.

With cats, the process is the same, but the fingers go over the cheekbones below the eyes. I then turn my wrist, tilting the nose upward. The mouth opens, and I use my middle finger to further pry the mouth open. I then place the pill on the tongue and push it in. If you try this, remember that you need to practice. If you do it too slowly, the cat will squirm free of the hold.

If you get a dog or cat that won't take pills, there are other options. One is to use a small pill popper. This holds the pill and lets you put it at the back of the mouth without getting bitten.

Liquids are generally easier to give, but it depends on the patient. In both cats and dogs, I tilt the head so that I can dribble the liquid between the teeth into the mouth. I find this less stressful than opening the mouth and squirting it in forcibly.

You can also get many medications formulated into flavored liquids or tablets so you have no hassle at all.

## Ear Drops

Ear drops, also called otic drops, are generally easy to administer. The only thing you need to know is whether you treat the flap or canal, or both. In the case of the flap, I put a little medication on it and the spread it with my finger, or apply it to my finger and then smear it on the flap.

If the medication is needed down the canal, I dribble a few drops in the canal with the nipple of the bottle high enough that I can count the drops, which is usually between two and four. More than this is a waste. I then massage the outer canal to milk the ointment down and spread it on all canal surfaces. Do not put the tip of the tube in the canal as you won't be able to see how much you are putting in.

Have you ever wondered about the the difference between an ointment and a cream? I did. An ointment has an oil base. A cream has a water base. That's all that it means.

## Eye Drops

Sometimes you'll be called on to give eye drops, also called ophthalmic drops. You can do this by having the drops ready and opening the eyelids with two fingers.

Once you are in position, squeeze the bottle so that a drop goes in the eye. Only one drop is needed. More than that will just overflow out the eye. If you have a tube, squeeze out about 1/4 inch (1/2 centimeter) on to the eye surface.

# Pet Sitter Emergencies

## Lost Pets

A pet sitter I know was looking after a tiny Poodle while the owners were away for two weeks. The job was going well. Rupert, initially terrified of her, was starting to come around. She had even petted him a few times. Her role was to feed him and let him out into the fenced back yard.

A few days before the owners' return, Lisa (not her name) went for her morning visit. She opened the door, just a little, and Rupert scooted by her and out to the street. Imagine how Lisa felt at this moment.

The problem was that Rupert had never been out on the street without restraint. He ran so fast that Lisa lost him a few doors down when he vanished into some shrubs. Because he was shy of people, he wouldn't come when called and he was very stressed being in unfamiliar surroundings.

Lisa did what she could. She went to each of the neighbors and told them about Rupert. She put up signs. She contacted the SPCA and vets. And, she spent as much time as she could looking for the little fellow.

Two days later, one of the neighbors told her that he saw Rupert. He'd tried to entice Rupert to him but the timid little dog wouldn't come close. This gave her an idea. She got a live trap and set it with Rupert's favorite food. It worked. He was hungry enough that he went for the food.

She returned him to the house, a day before the owners returned.

I hope this never happens to you, but in case it does, or in case it happens to one of your clients and you want to help, let's go over what you can do in such an emergency.

The most important step is being prepared in case a pet goes missing. Identification (ID) is the key. This could be permanent ID, such as a tattoo or microchip. Microchips are valuable because they are traceable no matter where you travel. They consist of a rice grain-sized computer chip that is simply injected under the skin. A reader picks up a code from the chip and this can be traced to the owner.

Tattoos are either those used by breed/kennel clubs which are used for pet identification in the show ring, or those used by local veterinary associations for lost pet identification. The first ones are difficult to trace because you'd have to contact the breeder group and the latter ones don't work out of the state or province where you live. If a pet stays local, they are valuable.

Temporary ID consists of a collar or harness with an ID tag. At my hospital, we engrave the rabies tag with the owner's phone number. It has helped many pets get back home. But, it is not permanent and can be lost or taken off by other people.

The other way you can prepare for losing a pet is take a picture of the dog/cat. If you have to generate a flyer or notice, you have something to work with. It's also helpful to write down a description of the pet - the breed, size, color, sex, and unique features such as a torn ear or strange hair pattern.

Lost Pets – What you Need to do

Let's suppose you have a missing dog or cat. The first thing to do is check the surrounding woods and ditches just in case he was injured. Go out at different times of the day rather than just after work. Keep calling and periodically just stand still and listen. It is hard to hear a weak cry or whimper from an injured pet. If you keep walking and never stop, you may miss the cat or dog that is timid and won't come out unless you crouch down and look "safe".

Most cats that go missing are recovered close to home, unless they travel back to a previous residence. For this reason, make a thorough check locally. Look under brushes, up trees, and in buildings and sheds. Ask neighbors if you can check their garage which may have been open just long enough to allow the cat in.

The next step is to put up a poster. These should be around the home and in prominent locations like local mailboxes. Include a picture, an accurate description, when and where the pet went missing, as well as a contact number for you. If you can, drop a poster off with the neighbors.

Phone the local veterinarians with a description of the pet just in case they treated a stray animal. This also puts them on the alert that you are looking for a lost pet. Many hospitals keep a lost and found book as well as bulletin boards. Also call the SPCA or local shelter and report the lost pet. Go to the shelter regularly so you can look for the pet because they may not match your description to the one they have in a kennel.

You can also place a lost pet advertisement in the paper. Include the information from the poster. Offering a reward is one idea some people use. I have mixed thoughts on this because I don't think rewards really work that well in this situation.

## Emergencies of your Own

Your clients are depending on you, so what happens if you are incapacitated? Maybe you fall and break your ankle. Maybe you have a kidney stone or the flu. There are times you may not be able to get out to clients' homes.

The clients you have booked are depending on you. They often can't look after their pets, especially if they are in Hawaii. This puts the onus squarely on you.

How can you solve this dilemma? You need someone to take over your job. Perhaps you have forged a relationship with another pet sitter. Maybe you have relatives or friends willing to help. If you have employees or a partner, they should be able to take on your calls.

Whatever you set up, tell clients as soon as a problem surfaces. If you can't call, get someone to contact them.

To be prepared for this event, you need to keep a listing of your appointments as well as files available for each so that someone can move in and help you out.

## Sudden Death of the Pet

It seems ironic that the moment I was writing this lesson, I got a call from a pet sitter about this very topic. She was staying at a home, looking after Baron, a boisterous eight-year-old German Shepherd. She's gone out at 6 pm and he seemed fine. She came back two hours later, and he had passed away. What should she do?

Because the owners were my client, I told her that I'd call them to relay the news. When I did, they were baffled, as I was, on why their dog had died. They consented to a post mortem followed by a private cremation where they got Baron's ashes back.

Interestingly, even though they were devastated with the news of the passing of Baron, they were just worried about the pet sitter and how horrible it must have been for her to come home to a dead dog. This is how most people react. They certainly don't blame the pet sitter for what happened.

The port mortem gave us an answer. Baron had died from a tumor around his heart. The growth had bled into the sac around this heart and stopped heart function. This can kill a dog in a matter of hours.

These situations are horrible when they occur, but there are two things you need to do, and both require direction from the owner. The first one is whether or not the owner wants to find out why their pet died. Some do and some don't.

An analysis of the body after death is called a post mortem. You have likely heard the term autopsy. This only applies to humans (auto means self). In animals, a post mortem is called a necropsy.

A necropsy must be done soon after death to be valid as the tissues will start to decompose (which accelerates in hot weather). A few days later is no good because the cause of death can be obscured. So, unfortunately, there is a time crunch on this and a decision must be made quickly.

The other question is what to do with the body. This is where you can help. If it's a small dog or a cat, you can wrap him in a small plastic bag, and though it sounds gross, put the body in the refrigerator. This preserves the body and prevents it from deteriorating and smelling. The plastic also prevents fluids from leaking onto other things.

If it's a larger dog, you have to handle it differently. You can sometimes put them in a large bag. If not, roll the dog onto a sheet of plastic and put him in a cool place to keep the body cool. On the garage floor might work well. If it's hot, you can put ice around the body. The other option is to call the veterinarian. They can store the body for the owner. They use a freezer.

Options for body care:

• Owners can bury the body at home.

• Veterinarians can organize a cremation. This can be done privately where the ashes are returned to the owner, or communal where several pets are cremated together and no ashes are returned.

• SPCAs and shelters may have crematory facilities.

• In some areas, there are private crematoriums.

• As well, there are a few pet cemeteries.

Losing a pet is an ordeal, but don't forget that you are there to do a job. To help the owner (who is likely away), you need to take control and sort out the situation. This may seem hard, but use people around you who are used to dealing with these situations. This could be a veterinarian, a friend, or someone at a pet crematorium.

# Muzzling Dogs

There are a lot of opinions about muzzles. Some people want them on every dog that walks out in public. They think every dog poses a threat. Others think muzzles are cruel. Let's review a few facts.

Muzzles are usually made of nylon fabric held on by a web strap and buckle that goes behind the ears. The wider part of the muzzle is put under the lower jaw. If you are unsure of how to put one on and, just as important, how to do it safely, either practice or get your friendly veterinary hospital to show you how it's done.

I'm often asked if dogs can breathe with a muzzle on. Dogs breathe through their noses, not their mouth. They can breathe. The only time you might run into a problem is when a muzzle is put on a short-nosed dog that has trouble breathing even on his best days. Think Pugs and Boxers. If you have a muzzle on one of these dogs and the dog looks like he is in distress, remove it immediately.

Basket muzzles made of wire or plastic are secured behind the ears with a buckle. Dogs can pant with these muzzles on so they can be left on a for a long time. They are useful for short-nosed dogs with breathing difficulties. These are often seen on aggressive dogs that are taken out in public.

This brings up a point. In some areas, certain breeds (such as Pit Bulls) have to wear a muzzle if out on the street. If there are laws in your area, be familiar with them if you are out walking dogs.

There are also times you may want to muzzle a dog. For example, if you want to do something and you're concerned about a bite. It could be cleaning an ear or trimming nails. If you are worried, use a muzzle for your safety. It makes the job go faster and it's not cruel.

# Health Emergencies with Pets

When animals are placed in your care, it's a good idea to get a veterinary release in case there is an emergency. I'll show you why this is important. Though the story involves a kennel rather than a pet sitter, the principles are the same.

A German Shepherd, being boarded at a kennel, was brought in late to my hospital one night. He was having difficultly breathing and trying to vomit. For those of you that have already guessed, the dog had bloat – a torsion of the stomach. He needed emergency surgery to be saved.

The owner was away and could not be contacted. The decision of what to do laid with the kennel owner. He really had no choice but to say "go ahead". We did surgery and saved the dog, and generated a large bill (several thousands) as the dog had heart complications after the surgery.

When the owner got back, he simply said "I wouldn't have authorized surgery and would have gone for euthanasia". He refused to pay and the kennel operator was on the hook for the costs. Remember this - as far as the veterinary hospital is concerned, it is the person who authorizes treatment who is responsible for the costs.

For example, if a dog is hit by a car and taken to the hospital by the person who struck the dog, the veterinarian will often do emergency care herself, but won't get into extensive treatment until someone authorizes it. As you can probably see, this can be a dicey problem when the pet needs extensive care and no one will take responsibility.

This is why it's so important to know the owners' intentions. I've provided a form on my website that we give to owners to fill out when they go away. The idea is for the owner to discuss their wishes with the person they name on the form. It is better if the one making decisions is not you so that liability falls on someone else. It should be someone you can call in the event of an emergency.

It's amazing what some people put on the form. Some want the total veterinary cost kept under $200. Think about this - it only allows me to examine the pet and euthanize it. However, most owners know what veterinary care costs and the form helps confirm that they are willing to have their pet treated. I had one client put a maximum of $1000 treatment costs on the form, for her pet rat.

And, how can you get the costs paid? Some owners go on holidays and leave a credit card number with the veterinarian or the pet sitter so it's covered. You can ask your clients to do the same with their veterinarian.

This makes a big assumption. It assumes they have a relationship with a veterinarian. If they don't, you may have to pay the bill because you have no option. So, your goal is to create options. Ask the owner for a credit card, or better yet, a friend who will pay the bill for them (the one named on the form) and they can straighten it out between themselves when they get back.

When you have an emergency, you need to know the following:

- What veterinarian does the client use?

- Can you use an alternate veterinarian if more convenient or after hours?

- Who makes decisions on the pet's care?

- Has the owner arranged payment for veterinary services?

- If a pet dies, what does the client want done with the body?

- Is there a favored groomer in case the pet gets sprayed with a skunk?

This is text I have taken from a pet sitter's contract and it sums up what we have been saying. You may want to include these words in your contract if you don't have anyone to take responsibility for the pet's care. Of course, the owner will have to sign such a contract for it to be valid.

Owner grants permission for Pet Sitter, at her sole discretion, to seek and obtain veterinary treatment for Owner's cat while the cat is in her care. The choice of a veterinarian for any medical care that Owner's cat may require shall be at the sole discretion of Pet Sitter.

Owner will reimburse Pet Sitter for any veterinary care or medical procedures obtained on behalf of Owners while cat while is in her care. Owner will reimburse Pet Sitter for any supplies (i.e. food, medication, etc.) purchased to provide proper care for Owners cat while in her care.

Here's one last tip. To help you in an emergency, make sure you've got a way to transport the animal. This can include pet carriers, pillow cases for cats, and leashes for dogs.

# Expanding the Business for Fun and Profit

You'll discover that pet sitting doesn't have to be just feeding and watering the cat or dog. As a pet sitter, you are perfectly positioned to add other services. This can include grooming for the animals you look after, cutting their nails, and brushing their teeth. Then there are services such as dog walking, puppy care and dog training, pet taxi, home sitting, and even poop scooping.There are other species to look after, each requiring their own expertise. The sky is the limit.

# Grooming

You likely aren't a trained groomer (if you are, you can add much more to your pet sitting service), but there are some basics you can do. If the dog or cat is long-haired, a daily brush helps keep them from matting. When you are doing this service, charge by the hour. You do not know how long it is going to take you. Combing out an Old English Sheep Dog is quite different from brushing a Jack Russell.

For combing out dogs and cats, use a comb that will get through the hair. You don't want to just brush the surface and miss the tangles down by the skin. The first time you go to comb out a long-haired dog or cat, you might have a pile of hair bigger than the animal. This is normal—many owners just don't put the effort into it.

When the owners says that the cat "has a few mats", this could mean combing a tiny clump out. It might also mean that the entire cat is one large mat and you will have to take a little off each day because the cat won't enjoy it.

Here's how I demat a cat. For small mats, I wiggle a metal comb between the mat and the skin and pull them off. If the mat is too large to pull off (and too painful), I resort to clippers. As I pull the mat, I shave the hair next to the skin. One thing to be aware of in old cats is their fragile skin. Their paper-thin skin (like that of an old person) can tear. Keep the clippers horizontal to the skin surface. It's easy to cut or irritate the skin if you pull the mat up, stretch the skin, and dig in with the clippers.

There are several good products that you can find at pet stores. Try a few to see which one works best for you.

The only parasite you can transfer between dogs (I've never seen them in cats) are lice. These little insects live on dogs and lay eggs (called nits) on the hair. You can transfer the lice adults or the eggs between dogs with grooming instruments.

Lice keep dogs scratching and biting. If you have good eyes, you can see the lice on the hair.

Fleas tend to stay on the host and you are not going to transfer fleas from house to house. If you transport pets, it is possible for eggs to fall off an infested host, hatch in your car, and jump on the next unsuspecting host. In areas where fleas are a problem, and if you routinely transport dogs and cats, you may want to ask your clients to have their pets on a flea preventive.

# Nail Clipping

Nail clipping is usually done every three to four weeks, so if you have pets for that long, the nails may need attention.

To trim a dog's or cat's nails (give them a pedicure), you need a trimmer. There are two types. One looks like a pair of scissors. The other, and the one I prefer, is called a guillotine cutter. You can also use human nail nippers in cats, but I find them fiddly to get into the right position.

I have many clients who won't cut their dogs' nails because one time they made one bleed. I'll tell you a secret - I sometimes make nails bleed too! In fact, if I don't, I figure I'm not cutting them short enough. I don't cut nails to make them look pretty; I do it so that the nails don't need trimming for a long while.

To make sure you do the best (and safest) pedicure, let's start with a look at some anatomy. The nail is made up of the hard nail on top and the blood vessels and nerves—the quick—underneath. If you cut the quick, the dog or cat will bleed, but he won't bleed to death. However, it can be messy and painful for the pet.

Cats normally have five toes on the front feet and four on the back. However, they can have more. There is one cat I see, and his name is Yeti. He has seven toes on each front foot and six on the back. (Yeti is another name for Bigfoot (or Sasquatch), so it's easy to see where he got his name!) This condition is called polydactyly.

Cats keep their nails retracted unless they want to swat you, so to trim them, you need to extend the nail. You do this by pressing down on the toe of the nail you want to trim. Once you have the nail exposed, look where the quick is. Cut the nail in the area where there is no quick so it won't bleed.

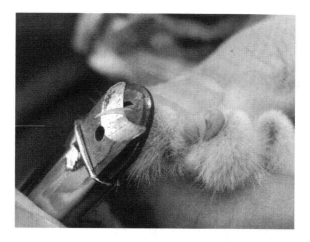

Dog nails can be tricky because rather than being white like cat nails with an easy-to-see quick, they can be black. If the nail is un-pigmented and you can see the quick, you can trim it like a cat's. If the nail is dark, the idea is to take small pieces off until the quick appears, and then stop.

The signal that you are approaching the quick is a change from a white chalky substance below the nail to a dark spot. The dark spot is flesh, so don't cut any further.

If you ever do cut a nail too short and it bleeds, you can use a silver nitrate cautery stick or a powder designed to stop bleeding. I tell owners at home that if they get a nail bleeding, run the dog outside so that dirt pushes into the nail and stops the bleeding. Alternatively, they can press corn starch into the end of the bleeding nail.

To be safe and make the job go quicker, use a muzzle if you need to on dogs. With cats, you may find you can do all four paws at once. For some cats, this is too much. Instead, do one paw, or even one nail, at a time.

# Dental Care

Brushing pets' teeth is coming into vogue. Some pets tolerate this well (they've been trained to do it) and it is an easy task. In others, it's a little more of a battle. Let's review the logic of tooth brushing so you can help your clients set up a program.

A dog's or cat's mouth is just like yours. Plaque (food debris and bacteria) forms on the tooth surface. If it stays there more than 24 hours, it mineralizes to tartar, also called calculus, which is a hard substance coating the teeth. When you go the dentist, s/he scrapes off the tartar that has accumulated since the last cleaning. Tartar on the teeth contributes to bad breath, bacteria constantly enter the blood stream and cause organ damage, and the gums recede so that teeth end up falling out.

This is the key. You must brush at least daily to stop tartar forma-tion. Some owners brush their pets' teeth once a week. This may make them feel better, but it does little for oral health.

There are many ways to brush teeth, but start with your finger and, once the pet is used to it, graduate to a finger brush or tooth-brush. Try to brush all the teeth, not just the easy to reach ones. Special toothpaste is available for dogs and cats with flavors such as chicken and tuna. Human toothpaste can be toxic to pets. Make brushing a nice thing for the dog (or cat). If you force it, the pet won't want it done.

# Dog Walking

Walking dogs has turned into a profession all by itself. I have many clients that hire someone to take their dog for a brisk walk. Here's the reason they hire walkers. One "little old lady" got pulled into a power pole (two black eyes) and then down (one broken hip) because her Bassett saw a cat and decided to go after it. These people may have balance problems or reduced mobility, but they still want to keep their dogs fit. Also, tiring out the dog keeps them more relaxed at home.

If you are the type that likes exercise, offer a dog walking service. The bonus – you can do more than one dog at a time. If the owners live close to each other, you can organize a walking route to pick up and drop off each one in turn. If they are farther apart, you may need to use your car to pick one up and then another.

How many dogs you can handle at once is up to you, but be sensible. Four to six seems to be the limit for good control. These dogs need to be well trained on a leash and able to socialize with other dogs. Not all dogs are suited for group walks. Group walks will take you between one and two hours, so you can't do that many in a day.

Some cities impose rules for walkers. One is that all dogs must be licensed. Sure, this is the owner's responsibility, but if you are caught walking and the dog has no tag, you may be fined for it.

Also, some jurisdictions require that dog walkers have a license. Check into the requirements for your area. Of course, obey all poop and scoop bylaws.

# Puppy Care and Training

Puppies create a whole new list of chores for the puppy owner, but this can translate into more business for you. The thing to realize is that they have tiny stomachs and tiny bladders. Fitting their eating and bathroom habits into a work day with the owner at the office just doesn't work. But, a pup needing a meal and a potty break in the middle of the day can work well for you.

When you arrive, plan on taking the puppy out right away. A quick meal might be the next thing to do, followed with a little play so they will sleep all afternoon until the client gets home.

To aid in housebreaking, some owners use crate training. This is a great idea as long as the puppy is allowed out when needed, which depends on the size of the bladder. You can learn all about puppy behavior and help your clients by giving advice on how to handle the growing pains (housetraining and biting, for example) they are going through.

I've put notes on the website below for you to learn about puppy training. Just click on owner downloads.

dogtraining.academy

# Pet Taxi

Pet transportation is another avenue you can pursue. While the owner is busy working, the pet may need to be taken to the groomer or the veterinarian. You already have a vehicle (unless you are taking public transport or walking) so this is an easy service to add for your clients.

Some owners depend on taxies, but if the dog is too big to put in a taxi, and especially if the dog is sick, some taxis would rather not transport them. This is where can come in, assuming your vehicle is large enough.

If you are doing this regularly, prepare your car. Some take out the back seats and build a platform that is sturdy and washable. You may want to have a stretcher that sits on the platform and can be secured in place. Of course, you will want to make sure you have a small carrier on hand to restrain cats and small dogs.

Some pet sitters take this a little further and rather than just supplying a ride, they offer water, treats, blankies, soothing dog or cat music, all in air-conditioned comfort. The rate you charge depends on your hourly rate as well as the cost to run your vehicle. Emergency rates should be double or more when you are asked to respond quickly.

Make sure your car insurance or pet sitting liability insurance covers pets you want to transport.

# Pet Boarding

Maybe you want to care for clients' pets in your own home. I'm going to start with reasons not to do this. Because pets like to be in their own home, your clients may prefer to have their friends in familiar surroundings. The other fact is that you are a pet-loving person and, chances are, there are already pets at your home. Putting a strange dog or cat into the home may not be a good idea.

So, why would you do it? If you had a dog with special needs, or the client's home was far away at the edge of your territory, it could be better for the dog or time-saving to you if you let them check into your home.

# Home sitting (staying in the client's home)

This is an idea you can consider, but it depends on what your home situation is like. If you have your own pets and they are depending on you to get home, this is not viable. But, if you are single with nothing to tie you at home, then consider it.

This means moving into someone's home while they are away for an extended time. If you do accept this job, make it clear that you still have a pet sitting business to look after and you won't be in the home all day long.

# Poop Scooping Service

I must admit I was surprised when someone said they were starting up a poop scooping service in my area. However, it has taken off. One fellow I read about now has three "poop" trucks on the road. His program is simple - he offers to come to your home once or twice each week and pick up the poop. He collects it in a large can on his truck which then gets emptied at the local sewage treatment plant. The time spent at each home is short so he does many in a day.

You can have a poop collection service as part of your pet sitting role or you can do it independently where you have specific days you go out with your equipment.

## Pet Massage

Here's another service you probably didn't think about – pet massage. There are many techniques, including T-touch (Tellington touch), Rieki, and muscle massage. This could be a quick massage while you are at the house on a visit, or it can be set up as an official massage session. Some jurisdictions don't allow massage of pets unless you are certified or are a veterinarian. Check the laws so that you don't run into trouble.

# Other Animals

The majority of your business is going to be dogs and cats. This is simply because of the numbers of these animals. However, you will get calls about different animals. Your life experiences often guide you in what animals you are comfortable looking after. You may have owned an iguana or pot-bellied pig, cared for a horse, or raised budgies or even guppies. This gives you a special expertise that you can use as a pet sitter.

But, what if you don't know much about the animal your client calls about? You can quickly get up to speed if you get on Google and do a search including the words "care of" and the species name. But, foremost, be honest with your client. Tell them what you know and what you don't. Most will be happy to tell you what care their animals need, and still employ you if you seem willing.

Most caged pets are kept confined and have very set routines. These include hamsters, mice, rats, and guinea pigs. Some, like hamsters and guinea pigs, are nocturnal, so you won't see much of them when you visit. You need to look for other clues that they are okay such as whether they ate and drank.

Several types of food may be used, but often, fresh greens are dispensed from the refrigerator. This is offered and replaced each day to keep it fresh.

Waterers should be cleaned and filled daily. Having two waterers ensures they won't go without if one plugs or drips out. The cage can get smelly and should be cleaned. Ask the owner where the clean litter/shavings are and how often they get changed. You will likely need to remove the animal from the cage. Ask the owner the best way to do this.

Rabbits might be used to running around the house several times a day or they may have an outdoor run for sunshine. Again, find out the routine.

The most common bird you'll see is the budgie (also called budgerigar and parakeet). But, you may also see finches, parrots, cockatiels, and exotics like lovebirds. Outdoor birds (turkeys, chickens, and ducks) may be part of your assignment if you are pet sitting at a farm.

If you are looking after things for just a weekend, you probably only have to supply fresh water and food. To do this, you have to put your hand in the cage. Make sure the bird does not get out or bites you. Do this with the owner the first time so they can give you tips on the workings of the cage. If the owner is away longer, you'll need to clean the cage. Again, get the owner to run through the process with you.

When it comes to birds, the main thing you need to look out for is temperature control. Birds do not like getting chilled; it can lead to infections and death. If it's winter, make sure the heating system is working up to par. To prevent drafts and give birds a sense of security, the cage is covered at night.

Many people have fish tanks as well as cats and dogs. The things you may be asked to do are:

• Feed the fish regularly.

• Clean the tank.

• Spot problems with the pump, filters, or temperature and fix it.

• Remove dead (and perhaps dying) fish.

The biggest mistake people make with fish is overfeeding. It fouls the water and poisons the fish. Only feed the amount you are directed to do. And, if you are changing water, only change 10 to 15 percent every week. There are many books on care of fish, and if they are going to be part of your routine, take a moment to learn about them.

Are you comfortable feeding mice to a ten-foot snake? Do you like tarantulas? These, and animals like lizards and scorpions, can be a challenge to your fortitude. I've had people ask me if I would look after a sick reptile. I just tell them that I really don't know anything about their care. If you don't want to handle these animals, you can do the same. If you want to look after them, ask the owner for instructions on what to do and get learning.

If you live in horse country, you may want to specialize in this type of work. You can use the same principles that you've learnt in sitting for companion animals. Schedule visits the same way and figure out your hourly rate.

With horses, you can add other services to the feeding and stall cleaning – grooming, exercising, training (if you are qualified), letting them out in the morning, and bedding them down at night.

The question that comes up when you are asked to go to a stable is —how do you charge? The same applies if you are looking after sheep, cattle or llamas. You could charge a visit fee to cover your driving and then an hourly rate. If it's winter and you need to do extra chores (such as cracking ice in the buckets), add a surcharge.

If you are looking after a barn, you may find that there are resident barn cats. As a stranger, they may not trust you and you'll never see them. They are like the shy indoor cat in this way. These cats have the same nutritional requirements and suffer from the same diseases as the "regular" cats you are asked to look after. However, people don't regard them as the same type of cat when it comes to veterinary care. This is where you need to find out what the owner's feelings are towards barn cats. Some will allow veterinary care. Others won't.

## Selling Products

The other thing you can do is sell products to your clients. You charge a mark-up as a profit, and the owner gets it delivered (assuming they see you often enough). This can include supplements, shampoos, leashes, and collars.

But, maintaining an inventory costs money. You can end up with a significant investment in goods that you are selling. Don't get into this unless you have a steady market for sales and can afford the investment.

# House Care

As a trusted person, the pet owner may ask you to do other things for them. These may be simple things such as caring for plants and gathering the mail while they are away. But, I've got one pet sitter friend who now does errands for the pet owner even when the owner is home. The client is usually an older person who can't get out easily. She goes to the store to get groceries. In one case, she picked all the apples off the tree for the person to can. The lady was elderly and scared to go up a ladder.

If you have clients that just hire you to take their dog for a walk at lunchtime while they are at work, there may be other things they can't get home for. For example, if you tell them you are available for home appointments (to let the fellow in to repair the dishwasher or furnace), you may find more work. But, don't get caught being there while someone comes in for a whole day of work. That's a property manager's job, not a pet sitter.